Doubtful Dictionary

by Douglas D. Drill

Doubtful Dictionary

by Douglas D. Drill

A compilation of unlikely facts
and improbable meanings and interpretations.

Edited by Roberta Wilson-Fulkerson
ILLUSTRATIONS BY KIM WILLIAMS

Career
PUBLISHING INCORPORATED
924 North Main Street • P.O. Box 5486 • Orange, CA 92667

ISBN 0-89262-023-4

2184353

Introduction

A definition, by definition, is *"an explanation of the meaning or meanings of a word; the act of bringing into sharp relief."* Now, what kind of sense does that make? In these troubled times, when I get a few moments of relief, I like it to be soothing, mellow, certainly not sharp.

That's why it's such a relief (again with the relief?) to browse at leisure through Douglas D. Drill's daffy collection of doubtful definitions. Here, a definition is not a stuffy, dry-as-dust explanation that tells it like it is (ugh!), but a zany, tongue-in-cheek description that tells it like it should be.

Look at it this way. By the age of eight, most of us know how to talk quite well. We don't need a dictionary to look up the meaning of such words as Psalter, ohm, or puncheon. Any child of six can use these words. "Jenny's having trouble with her food, Mommy," says the child, "Would you *Psalter* meat for her?" *Ohm?* Obviously, that is where you live. *Puncheon?* I heard a little boy use it just the other day when he yelled, "Stop *puncheon* me or I'll tell the teacher!" And while we occasionally hear a new word, it's easy enough to figure out, for example, that *twoscore* has something to do with a couple's sexual success, or that a *thunderhead* is a toilet with noisy plumbing.

This dictionary is designed to legitimize the real language that we speak every day and to popularize some of the lesser-known words of our language, such as *cribbage* (a vegetable which grows only in babies' beds), *buffalo* (a greeting to someone while in the nude), and *microbe* (an outer garment worn while speaking on a microphone).

The *Doubtful Dictionary* offers endless possibilities. Why not make it a part of your next party? Start by reading out several of the definitions; then offer a prize for the partygoer who comes up with the best set of daffy definitions within an allotted time period. Donate a copy to your local hospital. You'll soon have the patients in stitches. Kids — buy the dictionary for your parents. You'll be surprised at how smart they'll become in such a short time. Lovers — take a copy with you on your next date and impress the one of your choice with a few well-placed definitions. After you've ordered the champagne, tell the waiter, "No wait, hang the expense! Bring the real pagne!" Think how that will impress your date.

For you who are climbing your way up the business ladder, imagine how a few well-placed doubtful definitions can quickly and easily establish your reputation. At your next business meeting or convention, begin by telling your fellow *delegates* that they remind you of the double doors to a Jewish restaurant. Then, explain to them that the *chairperson* is the one at the end of the table wearing the wooden expression. If someone asks about the agenda, tell the person you don't care if it's male or female; it's all *neuter* you. If someone says, "How about a *discussion?*" say, "No, I'd rather hava dat cushion — da one at da end of da sofa!" When someone asks about calling the roll, jump right in with, "Here roll, good roll, butter come over here." I'll bet you never imagined what fun a meeting could be!

Read—enjoy—this is definitely the book for you. The world is becoming far too serious. *(Serious* – as in, "Switch on the TV, Dear, the World ⸺ just starting.")

A few words of caution, however. This doubtful dictionary of dubious definitions must definitely not be swallowed whole. Rather, keep it by the side of your favorite chair, or maybe on your favorite nightstand, and savor it (easy on the salt). Read just a few definitions at a time. And if you don't follow my advice, don't come running to me, complaining of literary indigestion! Finally, a word of warning: don't expect too much. *(Expect* – as in, "So I led her through the chicken yard, hoping to get my ⸺ .") The most a practiced punster or doubtful definitioner can expect to garner by way of appreciation is an anguished groan. *(Groan* – as in, "My how that boy's ⸺ .")

Happy reading. Welcome to the wonderful world of daffy, doubtful definitions. As for me, as soon as I can get this Bonaparte and Finnish my dinner, I'm going to popover to the local pub, enjoy a nice cool cascade and sing a few barcaroles: "Yes, we have no bonanza . . . ."

— Editor

a

aardvark – a difficult task.

Aaron – what the dentist tells the assistant before drilling, as in, "Please turn the ———."

abalone – an expression of disbelief.

abandon – tour, your television, records, etc.

abase – lower part of a lamp.

abash – quite a party.

abate – something to put on a hook.

abbey – writes an advice to the lovelorn column.

abbot – a well-known phrase, as in, "I wouldn't ——— any other way."

abdomen – male inhabitants of the land of Abdo.

abet – what you place on a horse.

ability – what a pelican gets after storing some of Lipton's bags.

able – a male bovine animal.

able-bodied – built like a male bovine animal.

abode – a small, open vessel with oars.

abolish – what you should put on your shoes.

abort – a good place to be in a storm.

abound – large leap.

about – prizefight.

about-face – what you look like after a prizefight.

abroad – woman (slang).

1

absinthe – not being present.

abstract – land purchased by Ab.

absurd – cattle belonging to Ab.

abut – posterior.

academy – your opinion of yourself after taking advantage of a girl.

acclaim – mining rights.

accommodate – going out with a communist.

accompaniment – the worth of a firm, found out after losing an account.

accord – musical sound.

according – musical instrument with keyboard and bellows.

accost – price (Italian).

account – member of the nobility.

accrue – those who operate a vessel.

accurse – popular Western beer.

ace – what you want on your report card.

achieve – head of a tribe.

aching – monarch or head of state.

Ack-Ack, ack-ack – sound someone makes while you're choking them.

acme – as in, "——— no questions and I'll tell you no lies."

acorn – painful growth on your foot.

acquaint – as in, "This is certainly ——— little place you have here."

acquaintance – the minuet.

acquaintant – a species of tiny insect which you consider to be pleasing, odd, or antique.

acquire – those who sing together in a church.

acre – a sore spot.

Acts – a tool for chopping wood.

actuate – something you might say to a sword swallower who became over zealous, as in, "How do you feel after that ——?"

acumen – those who assist in a game of pool.

acute – as in, "There's —— girl sitting at the bar."

Adam – expression used in the service, such as, "Up and ——."

adder – machine which sums up figures.

address – garment worn by women.

adenoid – as in, "I am very upset ——."

adhere – instructions on the blank pages of your math book.

adherent – one who follows the math book's instructions.

adieu – what you say when you get married.

adjacent – as in, "—— me to tell you to clean up your nest." (Spoken only between birds.)

adjoin – when you finally make that move to Madison Avenue.

adjourn – the opposite of adding mine.

adlib – Madison Avenue feminist.

administer – a Madison Avenue theologian.

admiration – used by backpackers when pooling resources as in, "How much do we have when you ——?"

admire – what you can fall into with promotional schemes.

adorable – amount of barter necessary when exchanging removable bits of your house for male bovine animals.

adorn – statement of unconcern as in, "I don't give ——."

Advent – a cloister for Madison Avenue executives.

advertise – something you do when you don't want to look directly at someone.

aerosol – the atmosphere of the sun.

affair – a countywide gathering of people to show off their produce and livestock.

affinity – amount charged by some golf courses.

affirm – company you work for.

affix – something you get busted for.

afford – one of Henry's automobiles.

affront – what you put on for some people.

aftermath – your next class period.

agency – body of water near Greece.

agenda – that which indicates male or female.

agent – opposite of a cad.

agile – a young human being.

agog – child's description of a canine.

agonize – what you get when your wife hits you in the face with an omelette.

ague – well-known spot in the Netherlands.

airborne – giving birth in a 747.

airforce – what comes out of your hair dryer.

airplane – the way you look before your beauty appointment.

air raid – what you smell after you spray for bugs.

airstrip – a process which renders you bald.

airtight – a drunk in a 747.

aisle – subject and verb as in, "——— take you home again Kathleen."

alabaster – statement by Al's wife as to his character.

a la carte – as in, "If you can't rent him a car get ———."

Aladdin – as in, "Don't wake up the maid, there's ——— bed with her."

alas – young girl.

alder – as in, "I ——— out in back of the barn."

alderman – as in, "I ——— outside and punched him out."

alfalfa – Greek quarterback.

algebra – woman's undergarment, covered with water-loving micro-organisms.

alienate – a science fiction term as in, "What happened when the ——— those people?"

align – what you get from your boyfriend.

alimony – well-known Sheik.

allay – someone who will go to bed with you (slang).

alledge – that which mountain climbers fall off.

allegory – description of a narrow passageway between buildings after a massacre.

allegro – as in, "This potion will make a leg shorter and this one will make ———."

allotment – "She may not say much, but there's ———."

alphabet – first money passed in a Greek horse parlor.

alternate – what the vasectomy will do to Nathan.

ambition – as in, "That was a rotten thing to do and yes, I ——— about it."

ambushed – an expression of exhaustion, as in, "Boy, I sure ———."

ammonia – as in, "You are a princess and I ——— man."

among – type of bean.

5

amount – what you ride upon.

amour – a Moslem person of mixed Arab and Berber stock.

ampere – as in, "I don't wear these clothes 'cause I'm a hippie; I really ———."

anaconda – used to be a cheerleader down at the high school.

analyze – as in, "Let's get a polygraph machine and see whether ———."

anchored – as in, "I want these apples peeled ———."

anchovy – used to be a cheerleader down at the high school.

Andrew – as in, "Slowly the gunfighter turned ———."

anesthesia – pretender to the Russian crown.

anger – as in, "Woman or not, Sheriff, she shot him and we're gonna ———."

animate – as in, "Well maw, I never thought we'd live to see ———."

annex – query as to the forthcoming patient by an Italian dentist such as, "Okay, who's ———?" (also pertaining to a previous spouse).

annihilate – proper question to ask when arriving tardy to a gathering.

answer – as in, "She doesn't want to see you ——— you will have to leave."

ant – your Mother's sister.

ante up – as in, "Good morning, is your ——— yet?"

antelope – as in, "I wonder what ever made your ——— with the stable boy?"

anthem – as the Cockney highwayman said, "I know you have the jewels, now ——— over!"

antimony – as in, "I may be against working but I ain't ———."

"Do as I tell you, or I'll Arapaho around your head

apache – as in, "You're not going to wear ——— dress like that, are you?"

apart – as in, "They've already finished casting and I didn't get ———."

apartment – as in, "Until you lose your hair, you never know how much ———."

apostle – as in, "You should rest for a moment; ——— make you feel better."

appeal – as in, "He fractured his leg when he slipped on ———."

appear – seasonal fruit.

append – that with which you write.

appendix – Richard's pen.

applesauce – used for cutting up apples.

appoint – as in, "You get to ——— where you just don't care any more."

appraiser – a member of the congregation who gets carried away with the spirit of the moment.

aqueduct – blue-green colored tube which channels heat from your furnace.

Arapaho – as in, "Do as I tell you or I'll ——— around your head."

arbored – as in, "This is a dumb party; we sure ———."

arc – an exclamation spoken when someone approaches.

archaic – what Noah had when he finally stepped off the boat.

archangel – patron saint of welders.

arctic – an affliction of the eye developed by welders.

ardor – as in, "Never darken ——— again."

aria – as in, "——— gonna keep 'em down on the farm, . . ."

arise – as in, "That should get ——— out of him."

8

armada – as in, "Have we introduced you to ———?"

army – as in, "Why would my enemy want to ———?"

around – type of song.

arraign – moisture which falls on your head.

arrange – where a Buffalo roams.

array – what Buck Rogers uses.

arrest – what you may need to take while reading this book.

arrow – as in, "Let's get out the boat and go for ———."

arsenal – as in, "His horse threw him into the pig pen ———" (British).

arsenic – Nicholas's posterior (also British).

arson – as in, "And have you met ———."

art – difficult or strenuous.

artichoke – as in, "I grabbed him by the throat and gave ———."

artificial – an officer of a museum.

Aryan – as in, "——— me are going down to the pool room."

ascend – the rear.

ascot – as in, "Mommy, Mommy, Johnny got his ——— in the revolving door."

askew – as in, "Why should they ———?"

assay – first two words of the National Anthem.

assent – smallest denomination of coin.

assert – something you take for your breath.

asset – more than one of a kind.

assist – what the doctor removes.

asthma – as in, "He started howling ——— grabbed him."

atlas – as in, "——— I've found you."

atoll – as in, "You could hardly tell she was pregnant ———."

atomize – a perpetual squint caused by peering into cyclotrons.

atone – sound in music.

attack – as in, "Watch this, I just put ——— on his chair."

attest – what you take at the end of a course.

attic – insect which bores under the skin.

attire – that which goes on a wheel.

attorney – used in golf.

attune – what you whistle.

aurora – that which comes forth from a lion's mouth.

auto – as in, "I didn't do it yet but I ———."

autograph – table for computing new car sales.

automat – what you place your feet on.

avalanche – as in, "Would you like to ——— with me?"

Ave Maria – Mary's street.

avenue – as in, "My skateboard broke and I would like to ———
one to replace it."

avocation – time off from work.

avoid – space between stars.

award – political section of city.

awe – what you say while the dotor is looking down your throat.

awful – how you feel when you have to say it too much.

axe – as in, "Don't ——— me that again!"

azure – as in, "I can ——— you that this will never happen
again."

b

Baal – what you pay to get out of jail.

baby – a honey-gathering insect which lives around San Francisco.

bacchanal – as in, "I just wanted to know if you were ———— that."

Bachus – as in, "If we go up against them are you going to ————?"

backbiting – a bizarre form of erotic foreplay.

backdrop – a button-down trap on the rear of long underwear.

backer – as in, "I think reverse has gone out, I can't ———— up."

backfire – in primitive religious rites, the act of pouring gasoline on and touching a match to the seat of someone's trousers.

backslide – going down a hill face up in the prone position.

backwash – what the nurse gives you in the hospital.

bacon – as in, "What's ———— in the oven?"

bacteria – crying so hard the tears roll down your reverse side.

badger – as in, "I ———— never thought I'd get here."

bald – what you did on your date last night.

balm – an explosive device.

Baltic – a small, hairless insect which burrows under the skin.

bamboo – on Halloween, a clout to the head followed by a shout, intended to scare the victim.

band – prohibited or forbidden.

bandit – as in, "The kids were getting too carried away so I —— in my house."

barbeque – the act of affixing sharp projections to the sides of your pool stick.

barber – one who barbs your cue.

barcarole – song sung in a bar at Christmas time.

bare – large ursine creature.

barely – behaving like a bare.

bargain – money made from selling a bar.

baritone – the sound your voice gets when you sing while eating a shortcake.

baron – as in, "Help, save me! There's a —— me."

baroness – Elliot, after Al Capone met him at the zoo.

barrier – one who sells bears.

base – horses of a reddish-brown chestnut color.

baseball – making love at the foot of a tree.

basis – as in, "If he rides the sorrel, you can have the ——."

bask – people from Northern Spain.

bassoon – as in, "If I don't catch a —— I'm going to take the boat back and go home."

baste – as in, "When I was in the army, I was —— in Georgia."

batch – group of bats.

bathinette – what you wear over your hair while bathing.

Bathsheba – as in, "Come on in the house, it's time for your ——."

baton – as in, "I say old fellow. Did you know there's a —— your head?"

bawd – slang expression meaning your person.

bawl – what you hit with a bat.

beach – derogatory term as in, "Son of a ———."

beagle – a tiny, white bird which flies around the ocean, gathering honey.

bean – a human.

beast – as in, "I wish you would ———ill."

beaten – pelted by a red, root vegetable.

bedrock – a popular dance performed while lying down.

before – as in, "See if you can catch that ——— me."

begonia – as in, "——— young rascal or I'll run you in."

behind – the posterior of the insect.

beleaguer – one step below little league.

belfry – one of the little known practices of poor Italian peasants who, if their prayers were not answered, would attempt to cook and eat their church bells (only practiced on Fridays).

Belgian – the act of ejecting gas from the stomach.

Belial – a small island shaped like a bell.

Belladonna – a pretty Italian girl.

bellhop – a dangerous game played by children in the church bell tower.

bellicose – dancing with your stomachs together.

bellow – as in, "The other bells are pitched high so you'd better make that ———."

Benedick – as in, "If I hadn't spent so much time pounding a beat I might have ———."

benefactor – as in, "Her habit of smoking dried banana peels in class might have ——— in getting her expelled."

13

belfry

beneficiary – as in, "If the kids didn't swim here this pool might have ———."

benefit – as in, "If you hadn't gained so much weight, Sir, this suit would have ———."

Beowulf – as in, "If he weren't scared of girls he would probably ———."

beryl – as in, "You must get out of the country, your life is in great ———."

beside – the part of your house which faces where the hives are located.

Bessemer – kiss me. (Spanish as in the song, "——— mucho.")

bestial – running off with another man's hives.

bestow – putting those hives somewhere on your own property.

bestride – using a wild animal as a steed.

beta – as in, "If you'd ever been fishing before, you'd know how to ——— hook."

betide – when the ocean comes way in and carries your hives out to sea.

betoken – a sting.

bevy – nickname for Beverly.

bias – as in, "If we're very good, will you ——— an elephant?"

Bible – purchasing a male bovine creature.

bicker – larger in size.

bigamy – as in, "Whattaya mean I can't marry two women? I think that's pretty ———."

bigotry – as in, "Hey, that's really a ———." (Italian).

big time – a very large clock.

bile – to heat a liquid until bubbles rise.

bilious – as in, "We'll take delivery now and then you can ———."

binary – as in, "I lost my lunch money and couldn't ——— a thing."

biplane – what a hijacker says while triggering an explosion.

birch – what a bird sits on.

bisexual – purchasing favors.

bison – what you say to your male offspring when leaving for work.

bistro – a queue of gargoyles, cyclopes, gorgons, centaurs and the like.

bitter – as in, "She kicked me you know where so I ———."

bitter end – (self-explanatory).

blackmail – masculine member of the negro race.

blade – as in, "I won her heart when I ——— my kazoo."

blanch – a woody extension growing from the main trunk or stem. (Chinese)

bland – a group of musicians. (Chinese)

blasphemy – as in, "I can't come with you to blow up the microwave tower so how about setting this last ———."

blaster – what your walls are covered with.

blaze – as in, "He doesn't sing well but he ——— beautifully."

blind date – a companion who has drunk too much and has to be taken home.

blunderbuss – a mistaken kiss.

board – wearied by that which is dull and uninteresting.

boardwalk – something which could happen only in a cartoon.

bobbin – as in, "Is it okay if ——— me go over to Joe's house?"

bobby soxer – an excerpt from a women's prizefighting match as in, "and with that ———."

boding – as in, "My cold is better now. Would you like to go ——— with me?"

bistro

bodkin – relatives who are allowed to touch your person.

boggle – a small bog.

bogie – nickname for a male actor (deceased).

boiler – what a cannibal might do when disenchanted with his current wife.

boisterous – as in, "They may seem like men to you but they're ———."

bold – as in, "I ——— 195 last night."

bole – what you eat out of.

Bolshevik – as in, "That's a bunch of ——— and I all saw him do it."

bolster – one who boles a lot.

bombard – dropping explosives on Shakespeare.

bombardier – a loss of hearing caused by dropping explosives on Shakespeare.

bomb bay – dropping explosives on the waters surrounding San Francisco.

bomb proof – the amount of alcohol necessary to withstand an explosion.

bonanza – as in, "Yes, we have no ———."

Bonaparte – as in, "I didn't finish my dinner because I can't get this ———."

bonfire – burning up your government paper securities.

bongo – from "The Owl and the Pussycat," "Where the hell did my ———."

bonito – a really great hobo.

bon jour – as in, "I haven't boned my fish yet, but I ———."

bonnet – as in, "I hope this horse wins, I just put twenty bucks a———."

booby – (self-explanatory).

booby hatch – a place to store boobies.

booby trap – when you notice a girl's chest and end up getting married.

boohoo – something said by trick-or-treaters.

bookkeeping – the practice of never returning library books.

bookmaker – a strange fetishism practiced only by extreme intellectuals.

boomerang – as in, "It's up to you," said the pirate. "You can either jump off the ———."

booze – sounds made by an audience indicating displeasure.

borax – tool which both chops and drills.

border – as in, "She asked me to take her home early last night. I think that I ———."

boron – as in, "Don't look at the pig pen, there's a ——— a sow."

borrow – from the old song, "Let's all step up to the ——— let's all step up to the bar."

Boston – expression of admiration for something weighing 2,000 pounds as in, "Say, that really is a ———."

botany – used only by androids and robots as in, "I went down to the shop today and ———."

both – hobos (spoken by a person with a lisp).

bother – as the nanny might say, "The child has eaten her dinner and it is time for me to ———." (English)

bottle – as in, "We went to the fair and ———lot of junk."

bottom – as in, "I didn't care how expensive they were, I ran right down and ———."

bough – as in, "I'm going back on stage and take another ———."

bouillon – as in, "Forsooth, let us go over and ——— terrible actors."

boulder – as in, "He came running into the house so fast that he ——— over."

bounce – as in, "My joy knows no ———."

bouncer – as in, "If she does it again ———."

bountiful – as in, "The County's not paying for wolves anymore we already have our ———."

bower – one who bows.

bowery – a place in which to bow.

box – swamps.

box elder – pugilism between senior members of the church.

boxer – as in, "Every night when I get home my wife and I put on the gloves and I ———."

boycott – as in, "And now in the local news, a ——— in the girls' dormitory."

boyhood – a young criminal.

boy scout – girl who goes looking for boys.

brace – one who is religious, as in, "He ——— every day."

branch – to soak in scalding water. (Japanese)

brandish – a casserole made from the skin or husk of grains of wheat.

brandy – not to be confused with brand X.

brassiere – a hearing aid made from an alloy of copper and zinc.

brass knuckles – a portion of a pig's foot found on certain metal statuary.

brass tacks – devices used to pin together artifacts made of brass.

bravely – performed by an adult male Indian, as in, "That was ——— done."

bravery – where warriors congregate.

brawl – as in, "If you lose any more weight sweetheart, your ——— fall off!"

brawn – as in, "She said she was going swimming and took off her ——— everything."

braze – as in, "Let us offer up a hymn of ———."

brazen – as in, "He must be going to heaven because he ——— everything."

Brazil nut – one who is crazy about Brazil.

breadboard – tired of making love.

breadfruit – to have encouraged copulation between apples, pears, peaches, etc.

breaker – one who stops a train.

breakfast – one who stops a train quickly.

breast stroke – (self-explanatory).

breathless – flat-chested girl.

breech clout – blow delivered below the belt.

breech loader – one who puts bullets into a pistol while it is stuck in a waistband.

bribery – school in which one learns to take bribes.

brickbat – a masonry stick used to strike a pitched ball.

bride – what you feel when you've accomplished something.

bridle – as in, "Never mind the bags, bellman, my new ——— take care of them."

brigade – cooling drink consumed by Navy prisoners.

brigand – as in, "They threw me in the ——— that was that."

"If you lose any more weight sweetheart, your brawl fall off."

brigadier – as in, "While I was in the ——— friend ran off with my wife."

brilliantine – a smart kid.

brine – what you think with (Cockney).

broadbill – your reckoning after a weekend rendezvous.

broaden – as in, "You've spent all your money on that ——— now you're broke."

broad jump – the act of leaping over a sleeping partner to get to the phone.

broad-minded – thinking of nothing but girls.

broadside – the part of the dormitory where the girls live.

brocade – an assistant without funds.

broken – as in, "I don't care I'm ——— that's that."

broker – as in, "She wrecked my golf clubs so I ——— jaw."

bronchial – a chocolate or coffee-colored timber in a ship extending from stem to stern.

brood – a person affecting an overly modest demeanor.

broom – sound made by exhaust headers and pipes.

brothel – as in, "Here, this cup of ——— make you feel better."

brotherhood – fellow member of the Mafia.

browbeat – to strike one's forehead.

brownie – indicates the color of the fifth letter of the alphabet.

bruise – as in, "Let's play leapfrog while she ——— a pot of tea."

brunette – cord, knotted and woven in an openwork pattern so as to keep overly eager people from falling into the vat while brewing beer.

brush-off – as in, "Quick, turn my ———, it's eating up my hair."

brusque – as in, "My hair never looks right no matter how much it's ———."

brutal – as in, "Oh my God, did you drink that beer? It ——— night and it's way too strong."

brutalize – a savage look.

brutish – saucer of beer.

Brutus – savage custom of the ancient Romans who, to make their beer, put us poor slaves into a vat and ———.

bubble – as in, "Come on, me and ——— walk with you."

buccaneer – a high price for corn.

buckboard – a dull and uninteresting feeling after seeing too many male deer.

bucket – a nasty expression indicating disfavor with something.

buckeye – a manner affected by Indian maidens in the spring.

Buckingham Palace – home of the official British rodeo.

buckle – as in, "Get behind a tree or that ——— run you down."

buckskin – a male deer's relatives.

Buddha – as in, "When the team came on the field we ——— long time."

buddy – from a famous World War One song, "Some——— else is sharing my trench."

budget – as in, "It's too heavy, I can't ———."

buffalo – greeting someone while in the nude.

buffer – as in, "As soon as the paint dries we've got to ———."

buffet – as in, "So the girls caught you in the ———."

bugaboo – scaring an insect.

buggy – a condition found in cheap rooming houses.

bulldozer – machine which encourages bulls to take naps.

bullet – as in, "We may have to get the tractor to ———."

bulletin – as in, "It's your fish, you ———."

24

bullion – small bull.

bully – a condition which occurs only to unlucky Matadors.

bulwark – cleaning up after a bull.

bumble – a bad or no good animal.

bumblebee – as in, "Where could that ———."

bumpkin – jostling relatives.

bunco – as in, "I'll never put a mattress like that on a ——— mine."

bunion – American folk hero.

bunker – an expression used to indicate that you intend to sidestep a tryst, as in, "I'm not going to ——— tonight."

buntline – direction in which the ball travels away from home plate during a sacrifice attempt.

buoyancy – as in, "I don't think that's possible, daughter. You'll have to spend the night with a ———."

burden – as in, "A ——— the hand is worth two in the bush."

burgess – as in, "I don't care who's dog brought it back! That's my ———."

burglar proof – indicates a powerful whiskey which intoxicates would-be thieves.

burial – to pelt Al with small, stoneless, juicy fruits.

burly – as in, "If you want my opinion, I think that you behaved very ———."

burner – as in, "Let's get that witch and ———."

bus boy – as in, "You'd better watch out for that ———."

bushel – as in, "It's teetering on the edge now. One more ——— do it."

buster – as in, "If your wife keeps taking my pot I'm going to ———."

bustle – as in, "Don't worry, the ——— be here soon."

bustling – a move to achieve racial balance in schools.

busybody – a money-making hooker.

butcher – as in the popular song, "——— hand in the hand of the man, etc."

butcher shop – as in, "Sorry Tom, I've got to ——— up for sale."

butler – in fraternity houses, a member whose job it is to deliver a swift kick to the posterior when you screw up.

butter – a male goat.

butterfly – as in, "Your wife shouldn't have worn those red jeans. The goat is about to ———."

butternut – one who loves butter.

button – what a goat does.

buttress – in sorority houses, a member whose job it is to deliver a swift kick to the posterior when you screw up.

buzzard – as in, "Today citizens of the county were terrified by an enormous bee which created a ——— for twenty miles or more."

buzzer – as in, "I think I'll ——— and see if she wants to spend the night."

bystander – as in, "If Ethel won't tell Aunt Millie Good ——— in the corner until she decides to behave."

C

cabbage – a cluster of cabs.

cabin – as in, "Hey, Mom, look in the backyard. There's a ——— our swimming pool."

"Hey Ma! There's a cabin the pool!"

cable – as in, "She is quite ——— of doing just that."

cacophony – as in, "John brought back——— won't be able to go on our second field trip tomorrow."

cactus – as in, "Yes Ma'am, the schoolmaster hit us and then he ———."

cadaver – as in, "Bring your trusty pistol, Watson. We can't let that ———."

caddie – a Scottish cad.

Caesar – as in, "When she comes out of the ladies room, ———."

cafe – as in, "Well, Hiram, I see you finally got rid of that———."

cahoots – the sound made by a strange bird obtained by crossing a crow with an owl.

Cajun – as in, "I don't know how your pet alligator escaped. I had him in a ——— everything."

calabash – as in, "Well if he's really gonna get married we oughta give ———."

calamine – used in the song, "Whatever happened to that old ———."

calico – as in, "Say, podner, where did that purty little ———."

callous – as in, "If you need any help ———."

calm – as in, "Oh ——— now. Things can't be that bad."

calorie – section of a theater with cheap seats.

calumet – as in, "What ever happened to that wonderful ———."

calypso – used in barber shops as in, "Please, this time don't ——— much off of the top."

camber – a box which fits into the bed of your pickup, equipped with beds, icebox, stove, sink, etc.

Camelot – place to buy used camels.

camel's hair – as in, "Hey, Yodar, your ——— again."

campaign – a bruise caused by being struck with a projecting, eccentric piece of machinery.

campus – the settlement cat.

canal – as in, "——— stay the night with me?"

canary – as in, "——— stay the night with me?"

canasta – as the Thin Man once said, "——— bring his bone into the house?"

cancel – as in, "If you lower the requirements I'm sure we ——— a lot more vacuum cleaners by Christmas."

cancer – as in, "I know you think that I can't support your daughter; well I ———."

candid – as in, "I took all of that moose you shot and I ———."

candidate – as in, "Bluebeard, in an effort to preserve his women for the future once ———."

candied – title to property which is written on a can.

candle – a preparation which removes the shine from cans.

candy – as in, "——— and I play doctor in the garage?"

cane – killed Abel.

canister – as in, "I ——— this porridge any longer." (Scottish)

cannibal – a process for preserving golf balls.

canopy – a container of preserved vegetable of the genus pisum.

cantaloupe – as in, "Sure I want to get rid of you Ingrid, but you ——— tonight!"

cantankerous – like, or having the qualities of a sailor who spends all of his time on destroyers and oilcarriers.

canteen – as in, "Birth control pills are all very well, but ——— age girls remember to take the damn things?"

Canterbury – as in, "If she insists on growing her own fruits, —— vines be planted on the other side of the barn?"

cantilever – as in, "I know it's difficult for the operator to reach, but why —— be installed right here?"

cantor – the act of being frank, open, or fair-minded.

canyon – as in, "What ho, Sir, —— fair maiden be the one?"

capable – what the matador does in desperation after dropping his sword.

capacity – as in, "Yes, you —— bag down to me if you'd like to."

caper – one who makes capes.

capital – as in, "No, I don't like to wear a ——."

capitalize – a disease of the optic nerve prevalent among reporters in Washington, D.C.

capitol – as in, "And then to —— off, she said that you were lousy at making love."

capon – as in, "One moment, my lady, and I'll throw my —— the puddle for you to walk over."

Capricorn – a vegetable grown on a sunny isle off the coast of Italy.

capstan – a place to hang headgear.

capsule – Korean headgear.

captaincy – as in, "I don't know if we've brought in oil or natural gas. We'll have to get the well ——."

captor – as in, "I —— in stitches all evening."

caramel – as in, "She wasn't a very good housekeeper but she took good ——."

caravan – as in, "It was on the Godfather's orders that I took ——."

caraway – as in, "One puff on this and it will float all your _____."

carbine – as in, "All right Martha. Where have you and that _____."

carbolic – a substance used to muddle up your car.

carbuncle – a bed made up in a car.

carburetor – as in, "As far as the missing pig goes, I think that _____."

card – run over by a car.

cardinal – run over by a car after having other things done to you.

cardiographic – a vivid description of an automobile.

cargo – as in, "Where the hell did my _____."

carmine – as in, "This is the final payment and that makes the _____."

carnation – the United States.

carpet – fooling around with a girl in the back seat.

carpetbagger – police officer who catches couples fooling around in cars.

carrier – as in, "She got so drunk that I had to _____ all the way home."

carrion – as in, "_____ my good fellow."

carry – having many cares.

cartel – a motel for people who ride in carts.

carton – as in, "Don't just stand there. Can't you see there's a _____ me?"

cartoon – song made up while driving.

cartridge – summit of a hill in the Old West where people abandoned their conveyances.

cascade – drink made by grinding up old wine containers.

cashew – a sneeze.

cashier – a condition of the side of the head caused by carrying your money in your ear muffs.

cashmere – as in, "It is only ——— money is all that it is."

castilian – one who steals casts.

castle – a mold in which casts are made.

castrate – price for having a cast made.

casual – as in, "The reason Ah came back is because Ah ———" (Southern slang).

catacomb – as in, "If she keeps shedding, for Christmas I'm going to give the ———."

catamount – to ride upon a feline.

catarrah – as in, "You gave the ——— steak that I was saving for dinner?"

catatonic – as in, "You may give a dog a sedative, but you should never give a ———."

cat call – ringing up a house of ill repute.

catechism – a cat lick.

caterpillar – a supporting column for a house of ill repute.

catnip – as in, "What I can't understand is why did the ——— the mail carrier? That's the dog's job."

cauliflower – what lassie ate on her way home.

cause – sounds made by crows.

cauterize – as in, "It was at that very moment that I ———."

cease – a multiple of the third letter of the alphabet.

cedar – as in, "That ain't true because I ——— out behind the barn with young Jed."

ceiling – expression used by people who made their living catching seals.

celanese – as in, "If the slave trader won't buy your nephew, oh great one, you could ———."

celery – a swap meet.

celibate – exchanging fishing worms for money.

cellar – as in, "If your concubine is too frigid why don't you ———."

cello – a gelatin dessert.

cemetery – theological school.

censor – used as in, "He must really love his wife. He ——— on all kinds of trips."

censure – as in, "I hear that you ——— husband back to his ex-wife."

census – as in, "We better leave before the boss ——— off on another job."

centaur – as in, "How come you ——— copy of "The Happy Hooker" to your mother?"

centennial – as in, "As for money, if you ——— just be writing for more again next week."

center – as in, "I ——— my pet iguana to help patch things up."

centerboard – as in, "I ——— back to the lumber company along with the termites."

centering – that which is on the middle finger.

centigram – as in, "I was afraid she'd get busted carrying that much so I just ———."

century – as in, "I sent you letter "A" on Monday, letters "B" and "C" on Tuesday, letter "D" on Wednesday and I ——— on Thursday afternoon."

cereal – as in, "If you want to ——— action, Lad, join the Marines."

ceremony – as in, "When she told me of her condition I gave ———."

certain – taking breath mints.

certificate – a little known Knight of the Round Table.

certify – to add a commercial form of pectin.

cervix – Knight of the Round Table famous for inventing a well-known chest rub.

cesspool – as in, "My son ——— relaxes him so that he can study better."

Ceylonese – as in, "Queen Isabella, you'll have to find me some other ships. I can't set ———."

chain – Tarzan's mate.

chain reaction – the feeling Tarzan had when he first came upon her bathing in the nude.

chair – the ex Mrs. Sonny Bono.

Chaldean – as in, "If your CB receiver was busted, you should have used the phone and ———."

chamber pot – marijuana kept in the bedroom.

chamois – used in the famous old carwash song, "I wish I could ——— like my Sister Kate."

champagne – a fake headache.

chancellery – a vegetable with crisp stalks belonging to the famous old Chinese detective.

chancellor – the basement of Charlie's house.

chant – as in, "Never fear, I ——— be long."

chapel – as in, "If you stand on the corner long enough, Mother, some ——— come along and buy your pencils."

character – a thespian who solicits money for overseas packages.

chard – as in, "Liking their meat well-done, the Celts ——— their steaks to a golden black."

charger – as in, "If she admits that she was soliciting ———."

charity – betting pieces of furniture on your golf game.

charlatan – as in, "Yes, she was in the Bahamas for two months and that's what made ———."

charming – a blackened Chinese dynasty.

chasten – as in, "Aw, we were just ——— those girls around a little bit."

chastise – a male optical condition.

chastity – as in, "I know how you love golf, Merwell, but control yourself, it's ———."

Chaucer – as in, "He takes a big quid of tobacco, see, and he ——— up real good."

chauffeur – as in, "I saved ten thousand dollars to buy this car and now I have nothing to ——— it."

chauvinism – the act of pushing in a crowd.

cheapen – bird sounds.

cheap skate – a flat salt water fish which emits sounds like a bird.

checker – as in, "I think I'll go over to the girls' dorm and ——— out."

checkerboard – as in, "I don't care if she is the women's surfing champion. Before she comes in here she'll have to ———."

checkmate – bunking with a person from Czechoslovakia.

cheek – desert chieftain. (Hispanic)

cheer – something to sit in.

cheese – as in, "——— really a nice girl when you get to know her."

chemical – something funny.

chemistry – a woody, perennial plant with one main stem and side branches upon which women used to hang their undergarments.

cherish – one who likes chairs.

cherry – a French endearment.

chest – beaten at chess.

chestnut – one who is extremely fond of chess.

chevalier – as in, "Hey mister; for two bucks I'll ——— snow off."

chevy – as in, "We'll all get in, so don't get ———."

chew – as in, "Can I get ——— some more wine?"

Cheyenne – a timid or self-conscious girl.

Chianti – as in, "Uncle Ferd wants you to give me your ———."

chicanery – the art of understanding California people of Mexican descent.

chicory – part of the lyric of a 1940's non-sensical song.

chiffon – as in, "Call the watch master. We're going to need an extra ——— duty tonight."

childhood – very young criminal.

childish – prone to getting pregnant.

chili – very cold.

chill – one who entices people to gamble.

chime – as in, "This is a very strange book which ——— writing."

chimney – first name of a cricket of Walt Disney fame.

chinchilla – a bag of ice, worn against the upper throat on hot days.

Chinese – as in, "After you've finished polishing that silver I want you to ———."

chinook – a Jewish expression indicating that a person is an idiot or socially unacceptable.

chipmunk – brother of the order that chops wood into small pieces.

Chippendale – taking an axe to Mr. Carnegie.

Chiropractor – doctor who practices in the Egyptian capital.

chisel – as in, "A historical Spanish leader which ——— Cid."

chit – vulgar slang expression indicating disgust, form of manure. (slang)

chit chat – talking about manure.

chivalry – using a switchblade knife.

chive – as in, "It's just a little something which——— whipped up."

chlorinate – as in, "We finally found out what it was that ———."

choir – as in, "So Cedric, you wish to a——— my daughter's hand, eh?"

choirmaster – as in, "How much wisdom will I be able to a———?"

chokecherry – an attempt to strangle a tree.

choking – as in, "Oh come now, you must be ———."

cholera – as in, "All right now,young man. Did you really——— whore?"

cholic – one who uses a telephone a lot.

chopping – as in, "The stores are open, let's go ———."

Chopin – an act required of bedridden patients in hospitals.

chord – as in, "With one a——— they all rose and threw tomatoes at the stage."

chore – as in, "That's ——— problem."

choreograph – machine which plays back dance steps.

chorus – as in, "And of ——— you may go too."

chose – as in, "She always ——— off for the boys."

chow mein – food prepared in our northernmost, eastern state.

christen – as in, "——— me are going over to watch Aunt Budgie throw a fit."

chromate – as in, "Remember what the Captain said, 'You've got to get rid of that ———.'"

chromatic – one who is incessantly attacked by crows.

chrysalis – as in, "Just so you don't forget anything I gave ———."

chrysanthemum – used as in, "——— are coming over for tea." (British)

chubby – as in, "After he hooked the ——— fell into the water."

chuckle – a missing piece of pavement.

chuckleheaded – going straight for a chuckle.

chuck wagon – action of a dog's tail when anticipating supper.

churl – as in, "Watch——— language you beast."

churn – as in, "What's ——— is mine."

chute – to fire a gun.

chyme – as in, "This is a very serious project which——— engaged in."

cider – as in, "Along came a spider and sat down be———."

cinder – as in, "If she gives you any trouble ——— back to her husband."

Cinderella – as in, "If Etta doesn't work out we'll ———."

cinema – as in, "I can't do that to her. That would be a———."

cinnabar – a place to drink and consort with the opposite sex.

cipher – as in, "Well my girl, it won't do you any good to sit around and ——— him all day."

circulator – used in expression of the 1950s, as in, "——— alligator."

cirrhosis – one of the lesser known knights of the Round Table.

cirrus – as in, "Aw come on, be ———."

cistern – as in, "We could a——— be done sooner."

citadel – often heard at parties, such as, "Now there ——— group of people."

cite – as in, "I guess you're telling the truth she ———."

citric – of or about a city.

civilize – as in, "She may say vulgar things but she has ———."

clam – used in song from *The Sound of Music,* as in, "——— every mountain."

clamber – one who digs clams.

clammy – a feeling of having eaten too many clams.

clamor – what Hollywood is purported to have.

clandestine – a Scottish family.

clapboard – a device used by those who don't wish to injure their hands while applauding.

claret – as in "Okay, Muldooney, but you'll have to ——— with the chief."

clarify – as in, "Do you ——— kiss you?"

clarinet – in commercial fishing to free a system of knotted rope which forms a pattern.

class – a clear substance which is used for windows.

classical – a summons to begin instruction.

clause – Santa.

clavichord – a multi-toned note produced by striking the upper breastbone.

cleanly – as in, "Be sure that you get this room ———."

clientele – a tearful confession (Chinese).

climate – as in, "When I saw that mountain I knew that I had to ———."

closet

climax – as the mountain climber said to his pal, "No wonder you're winded. That was quite a ———!"

clinker – one who builds jails.

clipper – as in, "I was just showing her how boxers stand; I didn't mean to ———."

close – what you wear.

closer – one who dresses you.

closeout – as in, "If you aren't home by six I'm gonna throw your ———."

closet – small figure of Saint Nicholas.

clothesbrush – as in, "Me and the Artful Dodger 'ad a ——— with the law this morning."

clothes tree – in mythology, a tree upon which the superstitious people of that time supposed their garments grew.

clouded – as in, "He wouldn't shut up so I ——— him alongside the head."

clubfoot – a swelling of the toes caused by standing at the country club bar too long.

club steak – a meal prepared by cave dwellers, who, when they were unable to kill game, were forced to begin eating their weapons.

coal – a feeling caused by frigid weather.

coal bed – what you are forced to get into when you don't have an electric blanket.

coal oil – lubricant used to keep coal from squeaking.

coal pit – large seed found in the center of lumps of coal.

coal tar – sailor who shovels coal.

coarse – as in, "Oh of ——— I would love to go out with you, Miss Prunella."

coast – a haunt or spirit.

coaster – one who exorcizes haunts and spirits.

coast guard – garlic placed over the door.

coasting – looking for haunts or spirits.

coat of arms – jacket made to fit Buddha figures with multiple appendages.

coattail – story about a jacket.

coax – a six pack of a popular soft drink.

coaxing – downing a popular soft drink.

cob – a police officer. (slang)

cobalt – two guys who both made love to the same girl, at the same time. (slang)

cobbler – a turkey. (slang)

cobra – a joint effort or collaboration between two ladies undergarments of the upper body.

cobweb – a sticky filament spun by the rare Iowa corn spider.

cockade – a hideous drink made by grinding up roosters.

cockatoo – as in, "So that big rooster killed your ———."

cockatrice – three roosters.

cocker spaniel – dog which chases roosters.

cockeyed – as in, "We should have fertile eggs soon from the way that new ——— the hens."

cockhorse – a steed preferred only by leprechauns and the wee folk.

cockney – an affliction caused by having roosters peck at your legs.

cockroach – the butt of a marijuana cigarette which has been found to be attractive to roosters.

coconut – one who is extremely fond of cocoa.

cocoon – racoon which collaborates with another.

cod – as in, "I think that I have ——— a bad cold."

code – that which you may have cod.

codeine – two school advisors who collaborate.

codling – fishing for cod.

cod liver – one who lives only to eat codfish.

coffee – a condition of having a perpetual feeling in the chest which causes involuntary muscle spasms.

coffeepot – a mild drug which causes involuntary muscle spasms when its smoke is inhaled.

coffin – as the man said while watching the carpenter at work, "I hear that your wife's been sick. Is that her ———?" "No," replied the carpenter, "she ain't dead yet. This is a chicken coop."

cognac – small, hairy bovine animal of a conical shape. (Tibetan)

cognate – as in, "We're never gonna get this transmission put back together if you don't hand me that ———."

cohabit – garment shared by two or more nuns.

coiffure – as in, "It's not polite to belch after you ——— beer."

coincide – the part of the bus where George M. sits.

coleslaw – an unvarying sequence of events discovered and formulated by Clyde Cole, who stated that, "Finely sliced cabbage, when marinated in a mayonaise type sauce, and purchased at fast food outlets, will always be limp and tasteless."

colic – a disease developing from overuse of the telephone. Also a tuft of hair on the back of the head which refuses to lie down.

coliseum – an expression from a child's story when Lassie was almost stolen away, as in, "I know they got away but did the ———."

43

collapse – trying to sit on two of your male friends at the same time.

collar – as in, "If she doesn't get here soon I'll ———."

collate – as in, "Okay, but we go to bed early so don't ———."

colateral – a pass to the side delivered by two quarterbacks at the same time.

collie – a use of the telephone often referred to by drunks, or by those who think they're being cute.

collier – as in, "It's past nine; hadn't you better ——— wife?"

Collins – telephoned reports by field units.

cologne – money which is lent with its return being guaranteed by two people.

colony – as in, "The referee will call the match if they kick each other but he can't ———."

color – one who scrounges up fruit which ripens on the vine.

colossus – when two people share a nonreturn of investment.

column – as in, "If the referee sees that player who lost his pants he'll ———."

comb – as in, "——— with me to the Casbah."

combat – a small, furry, night-flying creature used by Russia to deliver messages.

comedian – two politicians who share the middle-of-the-road policy.

comely – as in, "———, I don't think we're wanted here."

comet – as in, "Your horse became very excited and it took me an hour to ——— down."

comfortable – to be solicitous about a male bovine animal.

comma – used in the old New Orleans Blues, as in, "Won't you ———long with me?"

comment – as in, "After the battle begins anew you'll realize how much the ———."

commentator – an unrefined type of potato.

commisary – an apologetic communist.

commit – baseball glove used by communists.

commodate – an ordinary evening spent with a member of the opposite sex.

commodious – filled with chamber pots.

commodore – as in, "The front of the house boasted a very heavy iron gate, but opening into the foyer was only a ———."

commune – impervious to communism.

communicate – messages between communes.

communion – a joining together of communes.

compact – another word for detente.

compete – as in, "We're going to have a really great time. Why don't you ———?"

compile – heap of compost.

comport – Russian wine.

composition – job with the Russian embassy.

concave – a hideout for escaped prisoners.

conceal – as in, "Would you help me? I ——— this package."

conceit – as in, "It will be wonderful, I ——— now."

conceited – as in, "I don't like this catering to the prisoners at meal time, Warden. As soon as I get this ——— and his wine served, I'm quitting."

concise – a prisoner's height.

concur – the prison dog.

concurring – playing with the prison dog.

concussion – vulgar back talk from prisoners.

condense – as in, "I don't mind going out with her as long as she ———."

condition – as in a news cast, "Things went from bad to worse at State Prison today with the barricaded ——— up more than the guards could handle.

condor – as in, "If you really want to know how I got her to spend the night, I ——— into it."

conduit – as in, "It wasn't me, Warden. I saw another ———."

Conestoga – garment worn by Roman prisoners.

confederacy – a league or alliance of convicts.

confirm – business run by convicts.

confound – locating an escapee.

conifer – as in, "What did you boys do that to ———."

conjugal – as in, "Well, it appears to me as if that masked man ———."

conjunct – as in, "Where's that old Mongol wagon that the ———."

conjure – as in, "So that no good skunk finally ——— sister into marrying him, huh."

consent – as in, "Well Marco, did you get the leather shorts that Ghengis ———?"

conservatory – as in, "I may be a servant to a Whig but I never ———."

console – as in, "Where's that concubine that the ———?"

constitute – to play upon a horn without stopping.

contact – diplomatic negotiation with the warden.

contour – showing guests the penitentiary.

control – a gnome-like creature who lives under bridges in prison yards.

conventional – behaving like one who lives in a convent.

cookbook – an act performed in a fit of delirium by a librarian locked in the building over an extended holiday.

cootie – as in, "Hi there ——, remember me?"

copious – to cut out with a narrow bladed saw in a U-shaped frame.

coppery – a police station.

coquette – to cover with a popular soft drink.

coral – sung by a choir.

coral snake – one of the Clantons at the O.K.

cord – as in, "Would you like half of this apple that I just ——?"

cordial – as in, "As soon as the organ plays a ——, start down the aisle."

cordon – English general who was murdered by the Madhi at Khartoum.

core – a Cockney expression. (slang)

coriander – as in, "She said that —— were only going to the movies."

corner – one who picks corn.

cornet – that which is used to catch falling ears of corn.

Cornish – one who is fond of corn.

cornstalk – to pursue and hunt down corn.

corona – as in, "Why did you eat the whole apple and leave me only the ——?"

corpus – an unhealthful secretion in the center of an apple.

corral – as in, "If you don't give me that —— I'm going to go home."

correct – destroying the center of an apple.

correlate – as in, "She gave me the apple on time but she brought the ———."

corridor – to remove the center of a movable structure which closes the access to a room.

corrugate – to remove the center of a swinging framework which controls an entrance.

corsair – rough or unrefined oxygen mixture.

corset – as in, "Don't be silly, of ——— will work."

Corsican – as in, "She's a pushover, so of ——— date her."

Cortes – as in, "Well, Miss Borden, the ——— of the opinion that you did it."

cortex – as in, "Ah'm sorry, but the Sheriff says you got to go to ———."

cortisone – a lady in waiting to the French King. A prostitute.

corvette – as in, "The reason that boomerang isn't coming back to you is because you've got to ——— more."

cosmic – as in, "We didn't come home for lunch ——— picked a fight with me in the schoolyard."

cost – as in, "Your actions, Smedley, have ——— me to dock your pay."

costly – as in, "And that indiscretion ——— his job."

coterie – a place to purchase jackets and outer clothing.

cottage – a shop which sells collapsible beds.

cotter – as in, "Yep, this time I ——— out in the barn with the hired hand."

cotton – as in, "Well, to make a long story short, we finally got ——— they hauled us off to jail."

Cotton Belt – to strike with a bale of cotton.

cough drop

cotton gin – a popular drink in the South.

cotton mouth – a disease found in very poor families who attempt to eat their crop instead of exchanging it for food.

cotton tail – story about picking cotton.

cotton wood – as in, "Corn and 'taters wouldn't bring much of a price in that case, but ————."

cough drop – a medieval practice of throwing from the battlements people who kept others awake all night with incessant coughing.

countable – term the peasants used to describe a 16th century nobleman who looked like a male bovine animal.

counter – as in, "I'm sorry Sir, she was at the rear and we didn't ————."

counteract – as in, "I don't care for her personally, but I guess she might have some value if you ————."

countercharge – a fee for taking up a stool without ordering anything.

countercheck – a look to see how many people are being served.

counterfeit – a sharp display of feeling upon seeing your bill.

countermine – an explosive device used by anti-fast-food revolutionaries to blow up counters.

countermove – changing seats to avoid another patron's obnoxious behavior.

counterpane – a disorder of the stomach caused by eating lunch in cheap cafes.

counterpoint – a device employed by those who do not read English and have to resort to pictures on the menu.

countess – as in, "Now there's only five people to eat all this food, even if you ————."

county – endearing term employed by Dracula's girlfriends.

couped – being run over by a closed, two-door automobile.

coupon – as in, "For God's sake lower the bridge. There's a ——— the center section."

courier – an East Indian chef's assistant.

courtesy – as in, "We're all back, Lieutenant, except for Corporal ——— fell into the latrine and is taking a shower."

court-martial – as in, "Any other young fool who tries to ——— get a load of buckshot just like you."

courtship – a yacht belonging to the king.

cousin – as in, "Now there ain't nothin' wrong with speakin' your mind, but I don't hold with no ———."

coverlet – blanket rental.

coward – that which is toward a cow.

cowboy – as in, "You'd better get your hands offa that ———."

cowhide – a way to keep your stock away from marauders.

cowl – as in, "Watch out mister. That ——— run you down."

cowpuncher – boxer who trains with cattle.

crabby – a swimmer who emerges from the water covered with short-tailed crustaceans.

crackle – as in, "I'm afraid that if there's another earthquake that ——— swallow up the church."

crackpot – an expression meaning to partake of marijuana with someone as in, "Let us break bread, or let us ———."

cranium – that portion of the zoo where there are cranes.

crankpot – a type of narcotic made from hemp, and prepared by persons who are queer or eccentric.

cranny – your father's mother.

crape – a fruit.

crater – as in, "If my wife gives me any more trouble I'm gonna ———— up and send her back to her mother."

craven – as in, "He was so short that one day while walking through the cemetery, he fell into a ———— was unable to climb out."

creaky – property with many small streams of water running through it.

cribbage – a vegetable which grows only in babies' beds.

cribbing – making small, high-sided children's beds.

crick – sound made by a Japanese camera.

cricket – as in, "It makes a strange sound when you ———— together." (Japanese)

crime – dirt, grease, or filth.

crimson – the male offspring of the author of a famous book of fairytales.

crisis – as in, "They're out looking for the peeping tom now, so please don't ————."

crisscross – as in, "Santa has a lot to do on Christmas Eve, and that's what makes ————."

croak – a loose, sleeveless, outer garment. (Japanese)

crocodile – an earthen jar filled with a popular deodorant soap.

crocus – as in, "If the Godfather finds out that we hit his bag-men he's gonna ————."

Croesus – folds which are pressed into your pants.

crop – a vulgar expression as in, "All right you guys; knock that ———— off."

cropper – a pit toilet.

croquet – as in, "Okay Doc, so you think I'm gonna ————."

cross – as in, "I'll bet that my new success really sticks in your ————."

crossbow – an ill-humored weapon.

crosswalk – stomping along fretfully.

croupiere – as in, "The baby sounds a little ——than before."

crowned – as in, "Tonight we're having —— pigs knuckles for dinner."

crucial – as in, "If the Queen gets a good look at this —— abandon ship."

crucible – as in, "The First Mate isn't so tough, but the Captain of the ——."

crude – as in, "Yes, I —— once for the Harvard racing team."

cruel – a type of porridge.

cruise – as in, "The Captain will never come on deck with his 'Teddy' while the —— around."

crumble – a bad, or extremely undistinguished male bovine animal.

crusade – a refreshing drink served in the fo'c's'le.

crypt – as in, "I think that the barber —— me too close." (Japanese)

cryptography – the science of mapping subterranean cells or caves, used to inter bodies.

crystallize – falsehoods or untruths that can be seen through like clear quartz.

cub – as in, "I have such a bad cold I wish that I hadn't——."

Cuban – as in, "Yes Sir, the people from outer space got out of this little —— squirted us with water pistols."

cuckoo clock – a crazy timepiece.

cucumber – an actor who shows up on stage always at the right time.

cuirass – what the vet did to your donkey. Also an expression of reproach.

culling – as in, "Where are you ——— from?"

culottes – as in, "That's not true Benedict. I tried not to kick——— of times."

cumbersome – as in, "Many a starving actor has wanted a cue——— other person was eating."

cumin – from the popular song, "She'll be ——— 'round the mountain when she comes."

cur – as in, "It would never a——— to them."

curate – a doctor's schedule of fees.

curd – as in, "I'll bet that staying home once in a while never a——— to you."

curfew – as in, "If you show them that ——— people are going to want to buy any bulldogs from us."

curious – pertaining to a discovery of the renowned Polish scientist.

currium – as in, "If you take the children to a dryer climate you might begin to ———."

curl – a young lady.

curlew – as in, "Hey there's that ——— tried to kiss you at the dance last night."

currency – as in, "If you don't think he has fleas you just keep this ———."

custom – as in, "You bet I did. I ——— up and down."

cyanide – as in, "Scarlett knew the soldiers were looking for her. There was nothing left but to ———."

cyclone – used to be a track star down at the high school.

cylinder – as in, "Es gibt mit ein ——— vindow bottom." (German)

cymbal – a native name for a lion.

cynic – one who sins.

czar – as in, "Things haven't been so bad since ——— daughter ran off with the milkman."

Czechoslovak – as in, "They're having a contest at noon to see who can move the slowest and I'm going down to ———."

d

dachshund – as in, "I hope the boat gets back to the ———."

daguerreotype – as in, "She was so good that lotsa people would come to our Rome office just to watch ———." (Italian)

dahlia – as in, "Oh you great big beautiful ———."

dais – as in, "It had seen better ———."

Dakota – as in, "A cowboy never insults a pretty girl. It's ——— da West."

damage – as in, "I don't know what gets into kids today. It must be the ——— we live in."

damnation – a country bent on getting hydroelectric power from every waterway.

damper – as in, "No, you can't have a pony, we're too ———."

dance – as in, "Don't fool around with her, she's ——— girl."

dandelion – as in, "I don't know about the tiger, but that's really a ———."

dandruff – used to coach track down at the high school.

danger – one who believes in the philosophies of Denmark.

Daphne – a crazy joint, between the thigh and the lower part of the leg.

dapple – as in, "Yes, I sometimes ——— in real estate too."

dare – an expression of affection as in, "Yes, I do my ———."

dashboard – to throw a plank down violently.

dated – person who has eaten too freely of the fruit of the date palm.

date palm – where Arab boys and girls meet to go out.

datum – as in, "Yes, I like sorority girls, but I wouldn't ———."

daunt – as in, "——— you ever speak like that to me again."

dauphin – a sea-going mammal.

davit – as in, "Don't you dare speak like that, I won't ———."

dawn – man's name.

dead end – a condition caused by sitting on a hypodermic full of anesthetic.

deadline – one which fails to interest girls anymore.

dead pan – a deceased hospital utensil.

dead set – 45 minutes played by a band with no one in the club.

death ray – as in, "When you drive so fast you scare me to ———."

debark – as in, "With most dogs ——— is worse than de bite."

debase – as in, "You'll find a jug of whiskey in an opening in ——— of de tree."

decade – a cooling drink enjoyed on cruise ships.

Decameron – as in, "I would like to purchase ——— dat shelf."

decanter – a soloist in a synagogue.

deceit – as in, "I got up on the bus and gave a pregnant lady ———."

deceitful – as in, "I was unable to sit down when I found ———."

decent – as in, "The smallest denomination of coin in this country is ———."

decide – as in, "Captain, I think that de Mate just went over ———."

decimate – as in, "I know that he's a fine looking stallion but ——— well?"

deck – man's name.

declare – as in, "Okay boys, you can come out now. I think that we're in ———."

decomposed – to undo a musical composition.

decor – as in, "All right lad, stomach in, chest out. You're in ——— now."

deface – as in, "——— is de front of de head."

defeat – as in, "De head is on de opposite end of the body from ———."

defender – as in, "There is a big dent in ———."

defense – as in, "I don't want you kids climbing over ———."

defer – as in, "On a chinchilla ——— is de most important part."

deferred – what the baby did to the cat with Daddy's electric razor.

deficiency – as in, "I know you don't like sea food, but why don't you sample ———."

defile – as in, "Okay, who took the Adkins folder out of ———."

define – what you get from de traffic ticket.

definite – as in, "Maybe if we shout loudly at the bull we can ———."

deflower – as in, "De rose is ——— I like best."

deform – as in, "I don't remember de face, but ——— is familiar."

deign – resident of Denmark.

delegate – a swinging construction at the entrance to a deli-catessen.

deliberation – pertaining to women's emancipation.

deferred

delicate – a representative to a political convention.

delight – as in, "Turn on ———."

deliver – as in, "One of the most important organs of the body is ———."

demand – as in, "You better listen when he speaks 'cause dat is ———."

demobilize – disease afflicting people who can't bring themselves to see any other gas station but this one.

demonstrate – as in, "I hope the sign painters use the right size letters and get ———."

denature – as in, "It is ——— of de beast."

denounce – as in, "De adjectives are easy but not ———."

dense – a rhythmic movement of the body.

dental – as in, "If Fred takes my girl to the prom I'm gonna ——— his fenders."

dentist – one who makes dents.

denude – as in, "Many sculptors enjoy portraying ——— form."

depart – as in, "If I don't get ——— I'm leaving de theatre."

department – as in, "You'll never know how much getting———."

departure – as in, "Why did ——— hair on the left side?"

deport – as in, "Is it time, Sir, to serve ———?"

deprave – last words of the National Anthem.

depress – they who write about other people's activities.

derange – as in, "Home, home on ———."

derelict – as in, "If the team misses this field goal ———."

deride – as in, "They want too much money for this car, but I like ———."

derriere – as in, "I ——— to knock this chip off my shoulder!"

dervish – as in, "If you concentrate hard enough on what you want you may get ———."

descent – as in, "Soon now de hounds should get ———."

describe – one who writes.

desecrate – as in, "I don't think that I can get many more miles out of ———."

design – of the Jewish people.

despair – a wheel kept in the trunk of your car for emergencies.

despise – as in, "All right, corporal, unlock the prison. We're going to shoot ———."

detail – opposite end from de head.

detention – as in, "I may have to quit this job; I can't put up with ———."

detest – that which is given at the end of a course by de teacher.

detonation – as in, "It is strange to find that there is, owing us this large of a ——— with no appreciable resources whatsoever."

detort – something made by de baker.

detour – what you go on in foreign countries.

detract – what you buy from a real state agent.

detrimental – money owed which is affecting your mind.

deuce – money payed to belong to an organization.

Deuteronomy – as in "What did you ——— while we were hypnotised last night?"

device – that which de people enjoy six days a week.

diadem – as in, "Of course the drapes look different. I ———."

diagnosis – slanted parts of the face with openings for breathing.

diagram – as in, "Maybe we can disguise this stuff by changing its color. Why don't we ——— and see."

dialogue – changing the color of a portion of a tree trunk.

Diana – changing her color.

diaper – a person who dyes things.

diary – a place where you dye things.

diatribe – to change the color of a primative or nomadic group of people.

dice – as in, "I think that she ——— her hair."

dictaphone – as in, "I can't stand that thing ringing. Why don't you ——— in the cupboard."

dictator – a potato named Richard.

die casting – throwing strong pigments about.

Diesel – as in, "——— do very nicely, thank you."

diffuse – as in, "We'd better run as soon as I light ———."

digitalis – as in, "——— about the baby just to make us mad?"

dilapidate – to push your girlfriend off of your lap.

dilate – to hold on to life too long.

diligent – quite a gentleman.

dimension – as in, "Oh that's okay, ——— it."

dimple – a pole installed by the telephone company which hasn't enough light to be very visible.

dinky – a word used by drunks, as in, "How's about a little ———."

dinosaur – as in, "I'm sorry but this train has no ———."

diphthong – to immerse in liquid a simple piece of footwear.

direct – as in, "I think that the damn ——— my best sweatshirt."

directory – to change the color of the Minister's house.

dirigible – to play a funeral hymn for a male bovine animal.

disability – as in, "I must say, Sturmley, that ——— to get into trouble is going to cost you your job."

DISAPPOINTMENT

disappointment – as in, "Only the players in the game could realize how much ———."

disaster – to have relieved a woman of her donkey.

disband – as in, "——— can't even play in tune."

disburse – as in, "There ain't enough money in ——— to get me to fight a guy that size."

discord – as in, "When it's time to ring the bell, just pull on———."

discount – as in, "——— says his name is Dracula."

discourse – as in, "——— is a lot tougher to play than I thought it would be."

discrimination – to be able to tell one felon from another.

disdain – speaking of a person from Denmark.

disguise – as in, "I think that——— trying to put one over on us."

dishevel – something to remove snow with.

dishonor – as in, "If she feels naked tell her to put ———."

dislodge – as in, "I've been skiing up here for years and I've never seen a place in such bad shape as ———."

dismay – as in, "——— come as a shock to you but I have been living with your daughter."

dismount – as in, "No one in their right mind would go out riding on ———."

disorder – as in, "Hey, Sam, were you the one who took———?"

dispense – as in, "——— not writing very well."

dispose – as in, "Ask the photographer if he likes ———."

disproportion – referring to the amount of food allowed a professional athlete.

disseminate – to break up a theological school.

dissuade – as in, "I like leather jackets but —— is difficult to keep clean."

diurnal – to color a chamber pot.

divan – to color a closed truck, or one that has an enclosed bed.

divine – as in, "Yes, I sometimes enjoy a little fruit of ——."

diving bell – an attractive or popular girl who enjoys swimming beneath the water.

diving board – finding swimming beneath the water dull and uninteresting.

diving suit – being stopped from diving by a legal action.

Dixie – as in, "Did —— me when I stepped out of the shower with the door open?"

dizzy – as in, "He doesn't really think that I'll marry him, ——?"

doctor – as in, "I could tell he was a new captain from the way he ——."

document – as in, "I thought that you told the —— nothing to me."

doddering – having female children.

dodo – as in, "——, I don't really have a cold."

Doe – slang expression for money.

dog-eared – one who has had his ears chewed on by a dog.

dogma – as in, "I think that Junior just bit that ——."

dog tag – a game of football played with canines.

dogwatch – as in, "What makes that —— me all the time?" Also a timepiece for canines.

dogwood – as in, "Yours may not try to bite the mailman, but my ——."

dole – as in, "Why do you wear that —— sweater all the time?"

dollar – as in, "I'm going down to the saloon and see if I can find a ——— two."

domino – as in, "I told you that if he tried to see you again to tell that big ———."

donation – a country with lots of money.

done – a gray-brown color.

Don Juan – as in, "Yes, I used to make phallic symbols, but I haven't ——— in years."

donkey – used to teach music down at the high school.

Donna – as in, "I ——— wanna stay here."

doodad – from a verse in a Stephen Foster song, "The Camptown Ladies."

doodle – a cross between a deer and a poodle.

doodlebug – an insect which attacks these unfortunate creatures.

door – as in, "I don't know whether she smokes pot ——— not."

doorman – fellow who makes constructions for closing off the entrance to your house.

Doppelganger – one who belongs to the Doppel gang.

Dorcas – as in, "We'd better close the ——— my parents are asleep in the next room."

dormer – one who invades dormitories.

dorsal – as in, "She's getting so fat that it's difficult for her to get through ——— the time."

double – as in, "Look out for ———!"

double cross – twice as vexed.

double date – to eat two fruits of the date palm at once.

doubledecker – to knock out two opponents at once.

double exposure – two flashers going into their act at the same time.

double jointed – to own two bars.

double-park – two grassy, public areas set side-by-side.

doubt – as in, "I don't know if she's telling the truth, but I'm going to find ———."

douche – used at the end of marriage ceremonies as in, "I ———."

Douglas fir – as in, "What did you invite ———."

dowdy – to be informed on the current Industrial Average.

dowel – something to dry off with.

dower – place in London where people were imprisoned.

draft dodger – a member of the Los Angeles baseball team who dislikes keg beer.

draft furnace – used to heat up kegs of beer. (only in Canada)

dragon – as in, "How long is this meeting going to ———."

drain – what soldiers do in boot camp.

draughtsman – he who applies air to a furnace.

drawback – to sketch someone's rear.

drawbridge – to sketch a bridge.

drawers – people who sketch.

drawn butter – a sketching of churned cream.

draw poker – as in, "Okay, Hiram, take this stick instead of a gun, and if she starts to ———."

dray – a dreary day.

drench – a long pit dug in the ground.

drier – as in, "If you had so much fun with Etta last night then tonight I'm gonna ———."

drive-in – as in, "Believe me! That is no car to try to learn to ———."

driver – as in, "This ghost routine is going to ——— crazy."

drop kick – to complain about your sweetheart terminating your relationship.

dropper – as in, "If she kisses so lousy why don't you ———."

dropsy – a condition wherein one drops things continually.

druggist – an addict.

druid – as in, "I knew that was a picture of the man as soon as the police artist ———."

drumhead – a condition caused by poking one's head into a kettle drum while it is being played.

drunken – as in, "Boy, we really had fun at Sunday School today. There was a ——— the ladies room."

dry dock – as in, "Thanks for the artificial respiration. I'm going into the house and get ———."

dry run – going out for track on a good day.

dual purpose – to intend to incite someone to shoot it out with you.

ducat – a small duck.

duckbill – your reckoning after a dinner of the web-footed fowl.

ducking – to chase ducks.

ducking stool – avoiding a three-legged seat thrown at you during a brawl.

duck pins – fasteners used to hold ducks together when they come apart.

duelist – as in, "Of course it might be clearer to the committee if you ——— your grievances."

dues – as in, "Now here is a list of ——— and don'ts."

dugout – as in, "Well, there's room for Sal and Rose to get in, but that leaves ———."

dulcet – an uninteresting tennis match.

dumbbell – as in, "I was sleeping in the bell tower until someone rang that ———."

dumbwaiter – as in, "How did that ——— ever get a job in a place like this?"

dummy – as in, "I was going to bake a cake but, ———, I forgot the baking powder."

dumpy – a truck which unloads by tilting the bed backward.

dumpling – as in, "I never thought that the Chinese would ———."

dung – as in, "Okay teacher, I'm ——— now."

dungeon – used as in, "——— just love to see them get what's coming to them?"

dunghill – a manufacturing firm.

duper – follows super.

durable – as in, "Why would she follow aft———?"

during – used in the old song, as in, "He flies through the air with the greatest of ease. That ——— young man on the flying trapeze."

dust – as in, "And ——— thou love me then, my sweet?"

duster – used as in, "If my daughter gives you any trouble ——— backside with a paddle."

dustpan – a face full of finely powdered earth.

dyed-in-the-wool – found dead under a sheep.

dynamite – as in, "No, she's too prudish to let you do that on the first date but her roommate ———."

dynasty – to expire in an extremely vulgar way.

Easter Seal

e

eagle eyed – as in, "Food must be getting scarce around here. I'll swear that this morning an ——— me."

eardrum – a percussion instrument used by the rare Zamboula tribe of the Congo, and shaped like a human ear. Also as in, "This ——— ain't no good."

early – an endearing term used by his mistress.

early bird – a female ancestor of ex-President Johnson.

earring – a preliminary trial of a Cockney.

earwax – as in, "This ——— ain't no good."

east – as in, "A half pint of whiskey finally ——— my pain."

Easter – as in, "I ——— slowly over the cliff."

Easter Seal – an aquatic animal thought by children to bring them eggs on Easter morning.

easy – to have an abundance of the fifth letter of the alphabet.

eavesdrop – to fall off the edge of the roof.

eavesdropping – as in, "I think that your roof is rotten. I can see the ———."

echelon – as in, "When you're trapped on a narrow mountain ledge don't panic, just ———."

eclipse – as in, "The champion is still on his feet, and now ——— his opponent with a terrific right cross."

economy – as in, "I know that he's a con man, but why would ——— ."

Eden – as in, "I can't talk to you now, I'm ———."

edifice – as in, "The baby just told me that for dinner she ———."

edit – as in, "I found the last cream puff and ———."

eel – as in, "Any good Cockney knows that ——— never talk."

eerie – as in, "Oh, ——— comes now."

efficiency – as in, "Tom said that they're really biting down at the lake. I'm going ———."

eggplant – an agricultural practice of ignorant peasants who think that it's possible to grow chickens by seeding a field with eggs.

eggshell – a cartridge used to shoot at chicken coops.

ego – as in, "Which way did ———?"

Egypt – as in, "Let's face it sweetheart. ——— you."

eider – as in, "They'll never get their hands on this car. Let's ——— under a haystack."

eighteen – as in, "I can't help it, I just ———agers."

either – an anesthetic.

eke – a tiny scream.

elapse – as in, "I don't like that cat! It's the way——— his milk!"

elate – as in, "Boy, is ———!"

elbow – a Mexican weapon which shoots arrows.

elbow grease – lubricant for a Mexican weapon.

elder – as in, "She couldn't get away because I ——— by the hair."

El Dorado – the first two notes of a Mexican musical scale.

electrocute – a pretty or charming electrical device.

electron – behind the scene political bosses who select the president and vice president.

elegance – used to be a cheerleader down at the high school.

eggplant

element – as in, "I wonder what the hell ——— by that remark?"

elephantiasis – as in, "This is impossible! I know that your sister was found bound and gagged in the elephant's quarters, but how could an ———?"

elephant seal – a glue used to fold over and close elephants.

eleven – as in, "He may not be getting rich, but boy, is ———."

eliminate – to remove branches from a tree.

elixir – as in, "His wife may be tough, but I know that ——— every Saturday night."

ell – place where sinners go.

ellipse – upper and lower edges of the mouth. (Mexican)

elm – wheel used to steer a ship.

elope – as in, "The wolf couldn't run very fast, but boy could ———."

emancipate – top of a fellow's head.

emasculate – to become manly after fifty.

embalm – a nuclear device along with the "H," the "N," and the "B."

embargo – an expression which comes from listing gold alphabetically instead of numerically, as in, "Where did the ———?"

embarrass – a vulgar expression which comes from losing one's pants as in, "I ——— now."

embellish – pertaining to one who likes bells, as in, "I ———."

embitter – as in, "I don't care if she tries to make up, I ———."

emboss – as in, "I want you peons to remember that I ———."

emigrate – expression used by heavyweight title holder who went around shouting, "———? Yes!"

emissary – as in, "——— dear. I didn't know he was your cousin."

emptiness – as the Commissioner said to the head of the Al Capone task force, "So you came back ———."

emu – as in, "If I pet this cat will ———?"

encapsule – to put on headgear.

enclosure – as in, "When I get ——— perfume drives me crazy."

encyclopedia – to be within a one-eyed, pedal-powered machine.

endorse – as in, "No, you idiot, not the chestnut mare. I'm talking about the ———."

endow – as in, "I know I have to end this story, but ———?"

endure – as in, "Well, my boy. This should ——— little game."

enemy – as in, "If the Brotherhood finds out this will be the ———."

engine – as in, "It's not very fast but it keeps on ——— along."

engineer – a condition caused by being struck on the side of the head by a locomotive.

engrain – being stuck in a silo.

engraving – digging holes for interment in cemeteries.

enhance – as in, "Birds ——— are worth two in bushes."

enjoy – as in, "Come to the motel, my love, and let us be one ———."

enlarge – as in, "I prefer to deal ——— figures."

ensign – as in, "This freeway ——— two miles."

ensue – as in, "I don't care if he is your brother. I'm going to get a lawyer ———."

entail – as in, "Hey, let's get the car ——— those girls."

enter – as in, "I think that she wants to ——— association with us."

enterprise – as in, "I think that the scandal at the Mrs. America contest will ——— cake baking activities."

entrance – as in, "And now the swami will place himself ———."

entree – your breakfast in bed.

enunciate – a cannibal at a Catholic mission recalling what happened to the unfortunate sisters, as in, "All of the ———."

envelope – a small, deer-like creature who lives on the African plains.

epee – small green vegetable found in pods.

epic – a two-headed, metal tool used to break up rock, etc.

epicurean – relinquishing an obsession with a thin, pointed sword.

epigram – telegraphed message written on a thin, pointed sword.

epilogue – section of tree trunk wherein one sticks his thin, pointed sword.

epistle – a hand weapon rated number five alphabetically.

equilibrium – identical amounts of the same tranquilizer.

equinox – the same number of blows struck upon a door with the knuckles.

equip – a small joke.

erect – as in, "Don't ever invite 'arry again. Last year ——— our Christmas party." (Cockney)

erector – as in, "I don't know how this church can get along without any ———."

ergo – as in, "All right you scoundrel, let ———."

erode – as in, "He may be terrible at shooting but at least ——— well."

err – that which you breathe.

errant – that which your mother sends you on.

error – as in, "Are we running out of ——— is it just my asthma?"

escarole – as in, "Listen, I don't care how self-conscious it makes you feel. I'm starving, so run over to that baker and ———."

eschew – a sneeze.

escutcheon – as in, "Jimmy cut school today and now ———— hell from his old man."

Eskimo – as in, "If you want the answers to tomorrows test ————."

espy – as in, "Hey, are you ————?"

estrange – as in, "I'm glad that you warned me about him. He really ————."

ether – as in, "I don't think so————."

ethyl alcohol – used to be a cheerleader down at the high school.

Eton – as in, "I haven't ————in days."

etude – what Julius Caesar said to Brutus.

Eucalyptus – as in, "My mother said, ' Not so much off the top. ' Last month ———— too short."

Eugenia – as Aladdin said after he rubbed the lamp, "Is that ————?"

euphoria – as in, "When you bet on the other side Coach, it makes me wonder, are ————own team or not?"

eureka – as in, "I can tell that you found our skunk because ————."

Euripides – as the tailor said, "Hey, I see that ———— pants, eh?"

evangelist – one who manufactures vans.

even – as Adam said, "I think that ———— I can get along if she stays away from that snake."

evil – as the snake said, "———— be all right if she stays away from that Adam character."

exact – as in, "Yes, that was the sword swallower, our ————, that you met outside."

Excalibur – as in, "Oh no, we only use '45s' now. The '44' is our ————."

excel – as in, "Yes, gentlemen, I was a prisoner here for over two years, and this is my ———."

exchange – as in, "Remembering that she was no longer my wife, I gave her a full glass of Doctor Jekyll's formula and waited to see my ———."

exchequer – as in, "No, I don't work for Safeway anymore. I'm what you might call an ———."

excise – as in, "With this reducing plan I've lost over 240 pounds. What you are looking at is not the Goodyear blimp but my ———."

exciting – as in, "I don't mind my ex-wife being a cop. What I don't like is my ——— me."

exclaim – as in, "Yes, I'm the one who originally discovered this goldfield, and right there is my ———."

excretion – one who has lived on the Greek island.

excruciate – as Ulysses once said of the cannibalistic siren, "Hey, that was my ———."

execute – as in, "Yes, my ——— girl, but she snores."

exercise – as in, "No wonder you got divorced. I wouldn't want to have an ———."

exile – Atlantis.

exit – as in, "The mule wouldn't behave that way normally, but he ———on."

exorcist – one who jogs.

expander – as in, "I think that she's really neat but my ———."

expanse – old hospital utensils.

expect – as in, "So I led her through the chicken yard, hoping to get my ———."

expire – person who used to bake pies.

explain – where the Mississippi river now flows.

export – a town which no longer unloads cargo from the docks.

exposition – number 23 in the Kama Sutra.

expound – a place where they used to keep dogs.

express – an out-of-print newspaper.

extended – as in, "That's the bar that my ———."

exterior – as in, "That little dog looks like my ———."

eyelid – a hat that's several sizes too large and covers the eyes.

f

fabric – an expression of the 1950s as in, "I think that's just ———."

face – as in, "His insinuations didn't ——— me at all."

face guard – having to look at the warden.

face powder – a deteriorating condition of the skin found only on badly preserved mummies.

facial – an expression used by some southern senators, as in, "It's good to finally be standing here to ———."

fad – overweightness.

Fahrenheit – as in, "As a basketball player he was pretty———."

fairball – a light skinned, or blond, spherical object.

fair-weather – pleasant conditions for the exposition.

fairy – one who loves fairs.

faithful – as in, "If you like water I'll give you a ———."

faithless – to be anonymous in a crowd.

false – a cascade of water.

false bottom – a bustle.

falsehood – an undercover agent.

falsetto – as in, "These are worthless. They are a completely ——— coins."

falsity – as in, "You can't start a golf game with that. That's a ———."

Falstaff – bread which contains little nutrition may turn out to be a ———.

fanatic – to cool off the extreme upper portion of the house.

fancy – as in, "You'd better not strike me with that ———."

fanfare – cuisine served to stage-door Johnnys.

fanny – a small fan.

fan palm – to cool the inner surface of the hand.

fantail – to cool one's posterior.

fantasy – to cool letters of the alphabet, as in, "I ———."

farce – as in, "You know, Sweetheart, that I would never ——— you to make love."

farcial – as in, "I know my wife! She'll let me go, but ——— get mad."

farmer – as in, "There is ——— joy in giving than in receiving."

farmhouse – to plant crops within your dwelling.

faro – as in, "That's simply not ——— you."

farrier – one who operates a flat bottomed boat designed to carry passengers and automobiles.

farrow – as in, "It wouldn't be ——— me to take your money."

farthing – as in, "'Tis a ——— better I do today than that which I have done before."

fascia – as in, "I didn't come around before, Minerva, because I just couldn't ———."

fascinate – to do up Nathan's zipper.

fascist – one who moves quickly.

fasten – as in, "She may not see you if you move —— get here before her."

fatal – as in, "You'd better draw the shades or the sun will —— those expensive books."

fate – as in, "The ball was fumbled when the quarterback, Arnold Schleppenstein, tried to —— back for a pass."

father – used as in, "I don't want to drive any —— today."

fatuous – as in, "I would never have bought her a size eight if I had known how ——."

fauna – as in, "The mother deer gave the —— gentle shove."

faze – as in, "When he said that word to her she struck him in the ——."

federal – as in, "We were captured by a female cannibal and one of us had to go, so we ——."

feeder – as in, "If she doesn't come around I'm gonna —— to the hogs."

feelingly – as in, "After being run over by an enraged guinea pig, I wondered how you were ——."

fellowship – a boat sailing alongside yours.

felon – as in, "When I tried to jump over the bar I —— my rear."

felucca – as in, "I —— fool!"

female – insured letters.

fence – as in, "He is such a good swordsman that he can fight one man with the right hand while he —— off another with the left."

fencer – as in, "This statue we stole is too hot to keep. I'm gonna go down and ——."

fender – as in, "I'm gonna let you off with a warning because you're a first a ——."

fennel – an inverted, hollow cone, used to pour liquids through small openings.

feral – as in, "If you leave me here I —— die."

ferment – as in, "Please, lady, this restroom is —— only."

ferret – as in, "We are due for an earthquake, and I —— more than anything."

ferric – as in, "Thanks for asking. I'm only feeling ——."

Ferris wheel – the most beautiful one, as in, "You are the —— I have ever seen."

ferrule – as in, "The king enjoyed only a ——."

ferry – derogatory term denoting a gay male.

fester – as in, "I can't walk no ——."

festoon – a piece played very quickly.

fete – as in, "—— has thrown us together."

fetus – as in, "The baby had chubby hands and cute little ——."

feud – as in, "If we sent Olive away to her aunt's for nine months —— know what happened."

fez – as in, "Her body was covered all over with ——."

fickle – a cross between a fig and a pickle.

fielder – as in, "I —— hot breath on my neck."

field glass – that which holds your whiskey when you're away from the house."

fierce – as in, "I was afraid that all my —— would be realized."

fiery – not capable of holding onto good employees, hot-tempered, quick to let a worker go.

fife – number which comes between four and six.

fifteen – teenager who can drink an entire bottle of whiskey.

figurable – as in, "You know how a cow is going to act but who can ——?"

figure – as in, "What happened after that giant —— sister ate?"

figurehead – to pelt your head with figs.

filbert – as in, "That's enough food for me, but it will never –——."

file – as in, "She wants to know if —— spend the weekend with her."

filial – as in, "She'll —— full of corn pone and grits."

filibuster – as in, "You'd better take your hands offa that ——."

fillet – as in, "So you boys finally got to eat your ——."

filter – as in, "She don't like me no more ever since Ephraim —— mind full of stories about me and Drusilla."

filthy – as in, "I hope that these teachings will —— with knowledge, my son."

finale – as in, "The street doesn't look too good, but this is really a ——."

finance – as in, "How are your uncles and your two ——?"

finesse – as in, "You'll never bribe Capone with only a ——."

finger tip – to fondle money awarded for extra services performed.

finicky – five bucks for each lost door key.

finny – as in, "That's a —— story."

fir – as in, "Aw, what ——?"

fireball – a formal dance held at the fire station.

firecracker – person who works for the insurance company and investigates fires.

firemen – as in, "I know it's time for a tea break, but c'mon, we've got to put out this ——."

fireplug – to burn your chewing tobacco.

fireproof – a registered alcoholic content which is too low to be combustible.

81

fish ball

firetrap – a device which catches and burns up rodents.

firmness – to be totally in accord with your place of employment.

first fruits – certain ancient Greeks.

first rate – that which you get from a taxi driver before you start your trip.

fish and chips – a lunch of tuna sandwiches in a saw mill.

fish ball – as in, "I must have hurt your pet goldfish's feelings because I never before saw a —— ."

fisher – a crack in the ground.

fishhook–when a salmon catches you with a short left to the jaw.

fishing smack – looking for narcotics.

fish pole – a Polish carp.

fishtail – the act of shadowing or following after a fish.

fission – as in, "Nobody's here. All the guys from the atomic plant have gone —— ."

fissure – as in, "Where's that —— sister caught?"

fix – a small pear-shaped fruit, as in, "A large bowl of —— ."

fixture – as in, "Getting caught with that redhead really —— old man's wagon."

fizzle – as in, "Be careful or the —— bust you again."

flabbergast – a choice between being fat or drunk."

flagging – to cover with flags.

flagon – a cross between a flea and a dragon.

flagrant – sweet smelling. (Chinese)

flapjack – as in, "Okay, okay. Now what's all the —— ."

flapper – one who sews up the rear of long underwear."

flatboat – one that the bridge fell on.

flatbottomed boat – one which sat around the dock too long.

flatcar – one that an elephant sat on.

flatfoot – Floogie with the Floy Doy.

Flathead – a pot smoker who sits around a tenement all day.

flat tire – as in, "Doesn't sitting around here in this —— you out?"

flatulent – as in, "Did you make a lease agreement on that ——?"

fleece – small, wingless, jumping insects.

fleet-foot – a condition found in girls who are continually running after sailors.

flesh – what you do to a toilet.

fleshpot – dumping your stash into the toilet when you think you're about to get busted.

flippancy – as in, "I think that pancake is ready to turn. Give it a —— ."

flipper – as in, "Boy, your mom is gonna —— lid when she sees this house."

floodlight – as in, "Even if the dam breaks these new dikes should help to keep the —— ."

floorman – as in, "Hey, don't dump that trash on the —— ."

floorshow – as in, "If we get a smaller rug then won't the —— ?"

Flora – as in, "This house is really solid. Just stomp on the —— little."

floral – as in, "Okay, the chair recognizes that you have the ——."

florist – one who lays floors.

floss – imperfections.

flotation – used to be a waitress at the Jolly Spoon Cafe.

flow – a female's name.

flower – finely ground grain.

flower girl – a baker's helper.

flowery – covered with finely ground grain.

fluctuate – as in, "Well, I've been a welder for twenty years but I don't know what will happen to you after that ———."

flue – as in, "I just ——— down for the weekend."

fluid – a cross between a flunky and a Druid.

fluoresce – as in, "This ——— really slick."

flycatcher – supervisor in a pants factory.

foal – as in, "So you thought you could ——— me, huh?"

foamy – as in, "Is this letter ———?"

fo'c's'le – as in, "If you go around that way ——— think you're crazy!"

fodder – your paternal parent.

foe – as in, "What ———?"

foible – a tale by Aesop read by a resident of Brooklyn.

foliate – as in, "I think the cougar that has been attacking the horses is dead. It must have been that ———."

folio – as in, "The chimpanzee played polio, riding upon a ———."

follies – as in, "If he ——— me home from school again I'm going to scream."

follow – to lie uncultivated or untilled.

folly – as in, "She didn't listen, and by golly, now she's riding for a ———."

fondle – a small faun.

fondness – a liking for fauns.

football – an erotic form of love-making.

footgear – a system of shifting gear ratios without using the hands.

footman – as in, "Hey, get off my ———."

footnote – to write messages upon one's toes.

footpost – a mail service which only takes letters twelve inches long.

footrace – as in, "Are you going to ——— business venture?"

footscrew – (self-explanatory).

fop – sound made by a cork popping out of a bottle.

forage – as in, "Beauty be ———."

foray – as in, "The card says that this present is ———."

forbear – as in, "We're coming in loaded ———."

forbid – pertaining to an offer.

forbidder – one who offers this many points.

force – as in, "Why do you write your ——— that way?"

forceful – as in, "I'm sorry, Sir, you'll have to take room five as you'll find that ———."

forcing – making fours.

ford – as in, "This is more than I can a———."

forecast – as in, "Yes, nurse, this is my number ——— today."

forecaster – fisher who stands further into the river than his cohorts.

forefather – as in, "I know you're going to paddle me but what ———?"

forego – a town in North Dakota.

foreman – one who prefers a four iron.

forerunner – kid that you send to get your four iron.

forest – as in, "Sergeant, we'd better let the men stop here ———."

forestall – as in, "We have the number ——— at the Farmer's Market."

foreword – those words which one can't say on television.

fork-tailed – being attacked in the rear with eating utensils.

formal – as in, "And this song is ———."

format – as in, "I don't know what you'd want to do that———."

Formica – as in, "There were many prophets be———."

fortune – as in, "Okay fellows, let's play the number ———."

forum – as in, "They are a rotten bunch of kids and I can't feel sorry ———."

forward – as in, "Yes, I know that you're leaving, but for the life of me, I don't know what ———."

fossilize – as in, "I don't care what the Judge says, I think that the old ———."

foster – more rapidly.

foul – a bird.

founder – as in, "I ——— working in a cat house in Nevada."

foundling – as in, "Tell Honorable Grandfather that we have ———."

fourscore – an affair between four people.

fourth-class – as in, "Okay, I'll meet you after my ———."

fowler – one who works with chickens.

foxhole – as in, "Don't ruin the pelt, I want that ———."

foxtail – what a fox gets during mating season.

fox terrier – as in, "Did the ——— sweater?"

frame – a small fire. (Japanese)

franchise – used to be a cheerleader at the high school.

frankfurter – an open or candid sausage.

frankly – a Chinese shopkeeper.

fraudulent – as in, "What ever happened to that ——— your paycheck to?"

free – to escape or get away. (Japanese)

freebooter – one who feels no restraint about kicking you.

freedom – as in, "We just went into the prison and ———."

free love – what you're supposed to get when you marry.

free will – what a lawyer writes up for you without charge.

freeze – as in, "Working less hours ——— me for other pursuits."

freight – as in, "I'm a ——— that you are going to be disappointed."

friar – an airplane pilot. (Japanese)

Friday – as in, "This is going to be our biggest fish ———."

frieze – small, wingless, jumping insects. (Japanese)

frigate – as in, "If it doesn't work out, ———."

frontier – as in, "Why don't we lay the foundation for the———."

frugal – as in, "You been talkin' and talkin', now is you———."

fruitful – Fire Island.

fuel – a simpleton.

fulfill – as in, "I hope that you liked my cooking. Are you———?"

fungus – as in, "Let's go over to my place and have some———."

funnel – as in, "After you get married, my boy, your——— cease."

furbelow – as in, "His chest was covered with long hair and a lot of ———."

furred – as in, "This is not a one-sided issue as the Senator has in———."

fuzzy – to be overrun by a SWAT team.

g

gabble – as in, "If you keep on listening to those old biddies, Martha, all that ——— drive you crazy."

gable – an effeminate, male bovine animal.

gaggle – as in, "If you keep telling people that joke, one of these days that ——— get you into trouble."

gaiety – a light-hearted and happy afternoon snack.

gaily – as in, "Ever since I saw you in that kimona I've been wanting to ask you. Are you ———?"

Galahad – as in, "I know what you think, but this ——— the biggest bust I've ever seen."

gale – as in, "Why don't you gals come along with me and we'll just have a ——— time."

Galilean – as in, "Mister Chef, give my little ——— cut of that there beef."

gall – as in, "I've been sitting by the phone waiting for you to ———."

galleon – as in, "There's no ——— this ship."

galley – "Well ——— told me to watch out for his little girl, and that's what I'm doin'."

gallic – a strong-smelling, onion-like bulb used as a seasoning.

gallon – as in, "Hey Sheriff, there's a naked ——— your horse."

gallop – as in, "It's nearly five a.m. You'd better wake that little ———."

gallows – as in, "I don't care how big her husband is. That ——— me ten bucks."

gambit – to have sunk one's teeth into another person's leg.

gambol – a hollow, rounded container for washing one's legs.

game preserve – an attempt to score and beat the other team.

gang – a word used only by Robert Burns.

gangrene – as in, "When the paint dripped into the air conditioner it turned the whole ———."

gangway – as in, "Down here we take care of our own problems because that's the ———."

gantlet – as in, "I'm sorry but I ——— you in here dressed like that."

garden – as in, "Watch out, Louie. There's a ——— the corridor."

gardener – as in, "She's my little girl and I'm ——— from you."

gargoyle – a woman who likes garfish.

garland – where garfish abound.

garlic – to wash a garfish with the tongue.

garnet – a woven system of cords arranged to trap autos.

garnish – a Jewish delicacy made from a fresh water fish.

garrison – as in, "I don't ———, your Mother wants you in the house."

garrulous – as in, "I could———about your problems."

garter – as in, "Yep, I ——— to quit smoking, and to start drinking with me."

gash – what your car runs on.

gastric – something performed by magicians, using propane.

gauche – as in, "Well, how ——— the battle?"

Gaucho – as in, "Okay, Baby, I've ——— now."

gaudy – very religious.

gauge – a container for animals.

gauss – bovine animals from which we get milk.

gazelle – as in, "It's too late for you to interfere ——— and high water won't stop me now."

gazette – as in, "If you're married to me you gotta stop goin' out with other fellows ——— ain't right for you to do that."

gelding – as in, "I think that she's just ——— the lily."

gem – a man's name.

Gemini – as in, "Well, ——— thought that maybe you'd try it if we paid you enough!"

general – as in, "Perhaps in our next Olympics, Bruce ——— win another gold medal!"

generalize – as in, "I know, Señorita, that when the ——— a lady it means only one thing."

genial – as in, "If you give me your coats, my wife ——— show you to the parlor."

genital – as in, "No, I'm a whiskey man. I never drink ———."

genius – as in, "Well ——— guys thought that maybe you'd go for a pizza while we watch the game."

genteel – a gentlemanly water snake.

gentile – as in, "If you plug that ——— shoot out your lights, Hombre."

gentle – as in, "This here ——— show you to the bathroom, Miss Snidely."

geode – as in, "——— mule, let's get along home now."

Georgian – as in, "——— me are going down to the pool room."

geranium – what paratroopers say when they jump.

german – as in, "My Mother says that I've caught a ——— I have to stay in."

gerund – as in, "I kicked out his ——— he fell down on the floor."

Gestapo – as in, "The bus driver says that this is the big——— the trip."

gesture – as in, "I'll tell ——— not going with us."

Gettysburg Address – street number in a small town where John Paul lived.

geyser – as in, "It wasn't me that stole the lady's purse. It must have been some other ———."

ghastly – to be ill from inhaling gas.

ghetto – old cowboy phrase, as in, "———long little dogies?"

ghost – as in, "Well, that's the way it ———."

ghoul – as in, "If you walk in the swamp that ——— stick to your boots something fierce."

giant panda – as in, "The ——— movie of *Jack and the Beanstalk*."

gibbon – as in, "I've been ——— advice to folks for years and so far nobody's been takin' it!"

giblet – as in, "Captain, Captain, the ——— go and knocked poor old Smedley over the side."

Gideon – as in, "I really feel quite ——— a Ferris wheel."

gift-wrap – a coat that you receive as a present.

giggle – as in, "Never mind the long boat, Sailor, the Captain's ——— do."

gilding – forming a craft union.

gimcrack – as in, "No matter what they do to him they'll never make ———."

gingerbread – a bread made from a dough which must be very carefully raised.

gin rummy – a state in which the mind has become clouded by strong drink.

ginseng – to vocalize over the fermented fruit of the juniper.

giraffe – a beaker of wine.

giveaway – to allow someone to pass.

glacial – as in, "Mother says that if you don't put down that modeling ——— paddle you."

glacier – one who cuts plate glass.

gladiator – as in, "Even if she was your goose, Jeb says he's ———."

gladiolus – as in, "Yes, he's ——— saved his money."

Gladstone – a happy rock.

glamour – as in, "A mountain ———."

glance – such as the thyroid or adrenal.

glare – as in, "It's very ——— to me now that she never meant to come back."

glass – a group in which you receive instruction.

glassful – no more room for additional students.

glean – spotless.

globe-trotter – a round horse with a characteristic gait.

globule – as in, "If you eat that big ——— be sick."

glockenspiel – as in, "Okay, people. You will have thirty seconds to remove your clothes. So begin at exactly twelve by the ———."

gloom – a Chinese fellow getting married.

glucose – as in, "Don't fool with that crazy ——— it'll stick your fingers together."

glutton – as in, "The market shows a big ——— corn this week."

gnash – a car of the 1940s.

gnat – a man's name.

gnaw – slang for a negative response.

gnome – town in Alaska.

gnu – just produced.

goad – as in, "After that we'all ——— back down de road."

goatee – a small goat.

goatskin – relatives of a goat.

gobble – as in, "If you mess around with sailors, Beatrice, some ——— get you pregnant."

goblet – a small sailor.

goblin – as in, "At these prices the people are gonna be ——— up everything in the store."

godfather – as in, "Oh my ———, it's cousin Willy."

gold – knocked down by a goalie.

golden – as in, "I've got a ——— can't play today."

golden goose – sitting down on a 24-carat candle holder.

goldilocks – as in, "We'll never get in the house now, ——— the door every night at ten o'clock."

gold mine – as in, "Since none of you claim it, this makes the ———."

Gomorrah – a sleepy morning greeting.

goodwill – a very fine person named William.

gooseberry – a large, hard berry, placed on chairs by children so as to see their elders jump suddenly up.

goose-step – as in, "Let's get a ruler and see how far we can make this ———."

gopher – as in, "Okay, fellows, the coach says to ——— it."

Gordian knot – as in, "No, you idiot, this is a ——— an accordian."

gore – a Vidal point.

gorgeous – as in, "After the show they will ——— on other delicacies."

gorse – as in, "Of ——— we will be there."

gout – as in, "The goblins will gettcha if you don't look———."

government – as in, "Many people, from time to time, have wondered what George Mc———."

governorship – as in, "Well, your honor, it seems to me that as far as this here colony is concerned, you'd better start to ——— out."

grace – as in, "This is a good place for the horses to ———."

gradate – comes between grade seven and grade nine.

grade – wonderful, as in, "That would be ———!"

grader – as in, "She will do the test again, and this time I'm going to ———."

graduate – a cannibal after commencement, as in, "How was that ———."

gram – your father's mother.

grammar – as in, "My ——— told me that my father was worse than I am."

gramophone – to call your father's mother.

grampus – your father's father.

grandeur – as in, "Isn't it —— parents showed up for graduation?"

grandfather's clock – as in, "If I tell my grandmother about it that will really fix my ———."

granite – as in, "——— you have a point, but I still think that I'm right."

granny – as in, "I have looked in every nook and ———."

grapeshot – to fire a cannon loaded with small fruit—a procedure designed to embarrass the enemy, rather than injure them.

graph – a long-necked animal found in Africa.

graphite – as in, "These are very friendly creatures. You will never see a ———."

grapnel – as in, "I know where you've been all night, so don't hand me any of that ———."

grapple – as in, "That ——— mess up your mind."

grasping – trying to get one's breath.

grasshopper – one who makes love out-of-doors.

grateful – as in, "Before we light the fire you kids will have to clean out the stove. We've got a —— of clinkers."

grave – as in, "When we're not together I —— your company."

graze – colors that are a blend of black and white.

grease – what you have in your pants.

greater – as in, "I'm gonna get a file and —— down to nothing."

greatness – as the commissioner said when they put away Al Capone, "That was really ——."

Great Wall – as in, "If you think he was —— you just watch this."

Grecian – as in, "We'll be done —— your car in just a minute."

Greek – a stream.

greenhorn – referring to the color of an automobile's warning device.

gregarian – used to be a coach at the high school.

griddle – as in, "If you pour gasoline on your barbecue the —— blow up."

gridiron – a flat, heated metal plate used to press out football fields.

griffin – Attorney General Bell.

grime – a criminal act.

groan – as in, "My word, child, how you've ——."

grocer – as in, "He can help out some now, and of course the boy will ——."

groom – to be morose or dejected. (Japanese)

gross – as in, "I certainly hope that this plant ——."

ground hog – sausage.

groundless – as in, "We won't sell this much meat by next New Year's, you idiot. You should have ——."

group – a disease incurred by young children which causes severe coughing.

grovel – finely crushed rock.

grubstake – a long stick driven through the cook's plate by loggers, disenchanted with his work.

grumble – to break into very fine pieces.

gruesome – as in, "I was quite small when first born, but since then I've ———."

Gruyere – as in, "I see that you fellers have ——— own supply of pot."

guano – as in, "Bat ———, the most feared gunman of the old West."

guffaw – as in, "What did you take all of that ———?"

guilty – a drink made by brewing a fish's breathing organ.

guinea – a type of sack.

guitar – as in, "We're goin' to fix this varmint right now. Let's ——— and feathers."

gullible – to feed a sea fowl to a male bovine animal.

gumdrop – a place to get rid of your chewing gum before appointments, such as a letter drop in tall buildings.

gummy – a child who tries to chew too much gum at once.

gumshoe – a condition caused by stepping on chewing gum.

gung ho – a Chinese tool used to make furrows in a field.

gunning – cute or clever.

gunsmith – as in, "Okay, you'd better drop that ———."

gusset – as in, "No Sir, this ad was printed off the type that ———."

gust – as in, "Dis is one of de problems dat we dis ———."

gusto – as in, "I know that it's true because ——— me so."

guttersnipe – bird which lives along the eaves of your roof.

guttersnipe

guttural – as in, "I can't see the pig, have you ——?"

guzzle – as in, "If you aren't careful —— catch you with his wife."

gypsum – as in, "I give some people the correct change, but if I don't like them I ——."

gypsy – as in, "This whole thing has been a ——."

h

Habakkuk – as in, "This meal is terrible. Let's face it, we've got to ——."

habanera – as in, "You certainly —— mind."

habilitate – as in, "I hope to heaven that you —— for his portion of our expenses."

habit – as in, "Oh all right, —— your way."

habitable – capable of wearing a monk's robes.

habitual – as in, "Well, now if you boys would have listened to me, old Shep here wouldn't ——."

hackamore – as in, "Your cold must be worse, you're starting to ——."

hackle – as in, "If you stand in the street some —— run you down."

hackney – to chop at the main joint between the upper and lower leg.

haddock – as in, "—— listened to me this operation would have come off all right."

Hades – as in, "—— pictures came out good."

hadji – as in, "—— like to have a punch in the nose?"

haggard – an old woman who lags behind.

haggle – as in, "Watch out or that old —— cast a spell on you."

hagridden – as in, "Has that old —— her broom lately?"

hair – as in, "No Sir, she's not hiding in ——."

hairbrained – to have hair growing on the inside of the skull.

hairdresser – a chest of drawers made from human hair.

hairless – as in, "She's gonna be —— something happens to keep her."

hair net – profit made on a beauty shop, after expenses.

hair trigger – as Roy Rogers said, "I think that I ——."

Haitian – as in, "Most people —— to spend their money as quick as they get it."

half – as in, "I —— mixed emotions about this."

half brother – what you have after your sibling walks into a buzz saw.

halfhearted – a mistake by Doctor Barnard.

half-hour – as in, "Are we gonna spend —— lives just waiting for that kid to get ready?"

halibut – as in, "I woulda given him —— by the time he got home it was too late."

hallow – a greeting.

hall tree – as in, "Okay, Missy, you give me money, I —— away for you."

halo – as in, "Is it starting to —— what?"

halter – as in, "I —— all the way out to the dump and back."

hamlet – a small ham.

hammer – as in, "I don't know what I want for dinner, Dear. How about a —— something?"

hammerhead – a decision between a smoked pork leg and a ship's bathroom.

hammock – an imitation ham.

hamper – as in, "I'm sorry, Ma'am. Only one ———— customer."

hamster – one who deals in hams.

hamstring – used to tie up hams.

hance – the extreme end of the arms.

handbill – as in, "Will you ———— these latest reports?"

handcuff – having to hold your cuffs together when you forget your links.

handfast – a very quick movement of the hands.

handicap – as in, "Why don't you keep this ———— to cover your head with."

handicraft – a getaway boat.

handle bar – a cocktail lounge owned by the famous composer, George Frederick.

handsome – as in, "We know you have the gold in there, now ———— over."

hanger – as in, "The sheriff caught a witch and they're gonna ————."

happen – half a penny. (British)

harass – as in, "I wouldn't give her two bits for ————."

harbor master – as in, "Shall we destroy the infidel ships in the ————?"

hardihood – a criminal who survives many trials.

hardpan – extremely tough facial skin.

hardship – as in, "Captain, this is a ———— to sink."

hardwood – as in, "If this is too ———— you let me take it home overnight?"

hare – as in, "I wouldn't ———— of it."

harelip – a disease of the mouth incurred by kissing male rabbits.

hark – noise made in clearing one's throat.

harlequin – as in, "Go ahead and start clearing the table. ——— help you."

harlot – as in, "I guess that this was just ——— in life!"

harmonious – as in, "Tell the lady that ——— perfectly safe with us."

harpoon – a musical spoon.

Harpy – one who plays a harp.

harrow – as in, "Why, I wouldn't harm a ——— his head!"

harum-scarum – putting a fright into the Sultan's ladies.

harvest – as in, "We didn't find any of her other clothes but we did find ———."

hashish – as in, "As soon as I find my teesh I'll explain about him. He ——— own way of doing thingsh."

haste – as in, "We ——— them cows on up to the barn."

hasten – as in, "Yes, Ma'am, ——— the barn with Cousin Mary."

hatchet – as in, "Let's get a crocodile egg and ———."

haughty – as in, "How about a nice cup of ———."

haul – as in, "——— the King's horses and ——— the King's men."

hawse – as in, "Say that's a mighty fine looking ——— you're ridin'."

hawser – as in, "Gimme that ——— I'll tell the Sheriff on you."

haze – as in, "——— nothing but a big dummy."

headache – a continuous pain caused by waiting to use a Navy toilet."

headband – musicians who perform in the restroom.

headboard – as in, "I've listened to so many excuses that it makes my ———."

headdress – putting on your clothes in the restroom.

headhunter – one who is searching for a restroom.

headline – persons waiting to use the toilet.

headlong – as in, "Are you going to be in the ———?"

headmaster – man who has finally discovered how to work the flush system in the men's restroom.

head-on – as in, "Corporal Nutt, turn the lights in the ———."

headquarters – money to use a pay toilet.

headsman – fellow who services toilets.

headwaiter – person who is in line for a toilet.

heady – Lamarr.

heal – as in, "Wait on the Lord and ——— save you."

healing – what a dog does on command.

healthy – as in, "What the ——— doors don't open for a half hour yet."

hearse – as in, "This one belongs to you and this one is ———."

heartfelt – as in, "My ——— like it would burst."

hearty – a person with two hearts.

heavy-duty – being assigned to stand guard in a barrack belonging to the opposite sex.

heavy water – as in, "I'd like to ——— bed, but I get seasick easily."

Hebrews – as in, "Will ——— if I keep jabbing him with left hooks?"

hecatomb – as in, "What the ——— is a tomb, isn't it?"

hectic – as in, "What the ———, you've been president for six years anyway."

hedgehog – one who drives so far to the side of the road that he takes out the neighbor's privets.

hedgehop – a climbing vine used for flavoring beer.

heir – as in, "Let's go out and get some ———."

heirloom – as in, "Okay, George, turn on the compressed ———."

Helena – as in, "What the ——— couple of years no one will remember."

helicopter – as in, "I thought that I had the burglar covered, but ——— jewels and jumped out the window."

helix – as in, "I get mad at that old hound, but ——— my hand and I don't have the heart to scold him."

Helenize – as in, "——— my candy bar as if she wants it, too."

helmet – as in, "This was the dimension in which the forces of ——— the forces of heaven."

hemi – as in, "Would you ——— lift this table offa Cousin Clyde?"

hemisphere – to double and sew down the edge of a round object.

hemlock – a device to keep your hem from unravelling.

hence – female chickens.

henceforth – as in, "Sylvia will show her rooster third, and you can show your ———."

henchman – fellow who rang the bells at Notre Dame.

henna – as in, "Give that ——— hour more and dinner should be ready."

henry – a chicken coop.

hepcat – as in, "When you're under my feet all the time you certainly aren't much ———."

herd – as in, "I ——— you the first time."

hereafter – as in, "If you're not ——— what I'm ——— you're gonna be ——— I'm gone!"

hereby – as in, "This ——— is gonna turn out to be the smartest purchase I ever made."

hereditary – pertaining to the use of a henna rinse.

heresy – as in, "What would make ——— him again after all that he did to her?"

heretic – a blood-sucking insect characterized by the long filament-covered coat.

heritage – as in, "And this is a picture of ——— two, with her Teddy."

hermit – as in, "Okay, she can play left field. Where's ———?"

hernia – as in, "Hey, I see you looka my daughter's legs. You like a ——— eh?" (Italian)

heroes – as in, "And just for exercise ——— his boat about ten miles a day."

Herodian – one who rides in rodeos.

heroine – as in, "Yesterday we left our ——— an impossible situation."

heron – as in, "The customer claims, Sir, that he used our tonic, and now there isn't a ——— on his head!"

herring – what you have before a judge.

herringbone – to study up on what to say during the herring.

hers – a covered vehicle used to transport deceased persons.

hesitate – as in, "He won't be home for supper because he ——— with Judy."

Hesperia – as in, "He had a flat tire on the way here, but fortunately he had ———."

Hessian – sound made by a snake.

hew – man's name.

hexagonal – to be in extreme pain from a curse.

hexagram – a curse delivered by Western Union.

heyday – a time to cut and dry alfalfa.

hiatus – two victims of cannabalism discussing their demise in heaven, as in, "I think ———."

Hibiscus – small pieces of raised and shortened bread found at extreme altitudes.

hiccup – as in, "I've told you before, Daughter, when you're driving through those rural areas, never stop and pick a ———."

hickey – as in, "She's not very sophisticated. In fact, I think that she's a little ———."

hickory – a building which houses unsophisticated rural persons, rustics, or hayseeds.

high – a greeting.

highbred – a large amount of money.

high fidelity – remaining true to your marriage partner a large percentage of the time.

highhanded – keeping your arms over your head.

highjack – a greeting you should never use at airports.

highly – saying hello to Mr. Majors.

highpitched – of or like a tent on a mountaintop.

highway – a road traveled by Timothy O'Leary.

hillbilly – as in, "I knew you wouldn't like her, but what the ———, you're no prize either."

him – a song sung by a choir.

Himalayan – as in, "Certainly I know where my prize rooster is. That's ——— down over there."

Hippocratic – one who wants to change the Democratic symbol from a donkey to a hippopotamus.

hire – as in, "Can't you raise that thing any ———?"

historical – emotionally wild.

history – as in, "I can't see a Whig marrying one of the opposition, but if he must, then that's ———, and he's stuck with her!"

hit – as in, "What's ——— all about, Alfie?"

hogwash

Hittite – as in, "Although they're drunk, you should never ———— persons simply because they don't agree with you."

hoar – a prostitute.

hoard – as in, "If you think that you can come back into this house after you've gone out all night and ———— around, you're crazy."

hobby – familiar term of endearment for husband.

hobbyhorse – those who pursue prostitution as an avocation.

hobgoblin – quickly eating up hobs.

hobo – as in, "If you want this garden weeded you'd better hand me that ————."

hoedown – as in, "If you're going to be a Macy's Santa you'll have to get your ————."

hogshead – a toilet for porcine creatures.

hogtie – a swine worn around the neck and knotted to form a decoration.

hogwash – a carwash for pigs.

hole – complete.

holiday – as in, "It looks like a big pile of trash, but just a ———— and we'll soon be rid of it."

Hollander – as in, "I've been ———— trash in this city now for over twenty years."

hollow – a greeting.

holly – one who likes to haul things.

Hollywood – as in, "Ah so, you like to ———— for Chan perhaps?"

holocaust – an empty price.

holograph – an empty, long-necked creature.

holy – as in, "I don't ———— go along with you on this."

homecoming – as in, "The house movers just turned the corner and I can see your ———."

homer – as in, "I've got to get ——— my husband will throw a fit."

homestretch – to pull your house out to a greater size.

homily – parched corn.

homing – as the man said when he stepped into the rickshaw, "Take me ———."

honesty – as in, "It was ——— that I hit my first hole-in-one."

honey – an affectionate term for Attila.

honey bee – as in, "It's after midnight, oh where can my ———?"

honeycomb – a device with short teeth, used to make a hive presentable.

honeydew – as in, "Your honey may not keep you satisfied, but my ———."

honky-tonk – an armored vehicle with treads, filled with persons of the white race.

honor – as in, "Get ——— and stay ———."

honor system – as in, "I can't find anything wrong ———."

hooded – beset by thugs.

hoodoo – as in, "——— voodoo? You do?"

hoodwink – as in, "When I went by the poolhall I thought I saw a ——— at me."

hooker – (self-explanatory).

hoosegow – as in, "I say, ——— is this?"

hootenanny – a cross between an owl and a goat.

hopeless – as in, "I ——— people show up for this party than the last one."

hopper – a frog.

hopscotch – a whiskey produced in Scotland, and flavored with hops.

horehound – one who chases prostitutes.

horizon – as in, "If you get over to the cat house early you may catch a ———."

hornbill – a reckoning for repairing an auto's warning device.

horse – ladies of the night.

horseback – as in, "You'd better bring that ———."

horsefly – as in, "I've seen some strange things, but I never saw a ———."

horsehide – as in, "Now I ask you, where could a ——— in here?"

horseman – a fellow who is losing his voice.

horseradish – a radish that is losing its voice.

horseshoe – as in, "What ever happened to that ——— bought offa old man Peters?"

hospitable – as in, "This is good chewin' tobacco, but ——— is it?"

hostel – expressing enmity.

hotbed – a water bed with a thermostat run amok.

hotel – as in, "Chief say he know already that squaw pregnant, but ——— rest of tribe?"

Hottentot – to warm up a young child.

hourglass – as in, "Let us fill up ——— with whiskey and beer, and sing a song of Christmas cheer."

house – as in, "——— about loaning me ten bucks."

household – as in, "The flood won't wash away the barn, but will the ———?"

housemaid – as in, "I'm glad that we sold it. That ——— me work twenty hours a day just to keep it clean."

housetop – a spinning childs' toy in the form of a house.

howitzer – as in, "This is the story of ——— finally succumbed to his base desires." (from, "Arnold Witzer, A Study In Futility.")

howl – as in, "——— we get back into the dorm if the doors are locked?"

howling – as in, "Ancient Chinese proverb tell ——— kills great dragon and wins princess."

huckleberry – as Tom told Becky, "Just lay down on the sand and ——— you up to your ears."

huddle – as in, "The President thinks that ——— be the answer to our urban development problems."

huffy – as in, "She'll take good care of you boys and ——— will be only five bucks each."

Huguenot – as the condemned man said to the hangman, as he eyed the rope, "That's a ———."

hulled – as in, "Just ——— on to my hand."

humane – used to pump gas down at the service station.

humanize – that which homo sapiens see with.

humanly – as in, "It is these qualities which make ——— to my eyes."

humbug – a humming insect.

humdinger – a cross between a bee and a doorbell.

humdrum – an African drum which when struck sounds like the Mills Brothers.

humid – as in, "And there was ——— all the wise men, looking stupid as ever."

humidor – a warm, damp construction which closes off the access to a doorway.

humility – used to be principal at the high school.

humor – as in, "We should see Harriet and ——— often."

hydrophobia

humpback – a deformity of the spine caused by riding on camels.

hunch – a bunch of Huns.

hundred – as in, "How long I have ——— for your kiss!"

Hungarian – as in, "So, the next morning they ——— the rest of us headed back for home."

hunger – as in, "They took her out to the barn and ———."

hunky-dory – a Hungarian girl named Dorothy.

hurdle – as in, "No, I'm not going to her party. I find ———, and likewise her parties!"

hurl – as in, "Don't worry, ——— be all right!"

Huron – as in, "Hey, I saw ——— TV last night."

hurricane – as in, "All the other kids had some so I'm going out to the field and cut ———."

hurricane deck – weighted cards which can be used to play with out-of-doors in extremely high winds.

hurried – as in, "Since she took that course in speed reading I've seen ——— a whole book in ten seconds."

huskily – a manner of removing the outer covering of ears of corn.

husking bee – insect which lives under the outer covering of ears of corn.

hussy – as in, "——— returned yet?"

hydrogen – a juniper-flavored, alcoholic beverage produced in electrical generating plants.

hydroid – a stoned android.

hydrometer – from Greek Mythology, as in, "Yes, Ulysses, there at the end of this passageway will the ———."

hydrophobia – a fear of hydrants (found among some dogs).

hydroplane – a water-driven aircraft.

hymen – a bunch of stoned guys.

hymn – as in, "I knew all along that it was ———."

hyperbole – to be extremely 'up' for a league match.

hysteria – as in, "I just can't stand ———typed way of thinking!"

i

Iberian – as in, "I don't care, ———happy with you."

ice – that which you see with.

ice cream – what women put on before going to bed.

ice floe – as in, "You have the most beautiful ———."

Iceland – as in, "After someone blew up the ancient statue we found almost all of it again, but where did the ———?"

ice pack – as in, "Okay, put your ——— where they belong, she's married."

icicle – as in, "That's a dumb——— you're riding on!"

icing – as in, "You may not like my voice, but——— in the choir and no one complains."

icon – as in, "If you can go to the Yukon, then ———."

icy – as in, "——— said the blind man."

id – as in, "All that night we ——— under the haystack while they searched for us."

idea – as in, "Quick, while he's not looking let's ———."

ideal – as in, "No, you dealt last time. This time ———."

idealist–as in, "Well, I'll tell you one thing, if——— hand there'll be no cheating."

illegal

idealize – as in, "She had ———, one on each side of her nose."

identify – meaning, "I practice dentistry!"

ides – as in, "No matter where'e ———, we'll find 'im soon."

idiocy – as in, "Did that ——— which way she went, at least?"

idiosyncrasy – as in, "I don't want him in the choir. Ever since his operation something makes that ———."

idol – a greeting to a young lady.

idolize – as in, "If we keep sounding the lake we may find out at what depth the ———."

iguana – as in, "——— go home now?"

illegal – a sick bird.

illiterate – to be both sick and well-read.

illuminator – as in, "I hope that these teachings will——— mind."

immense – as in, "Women's rest rooms are usually much cleaner than ———."

immerse – as in, "He promised her that he would marry her and I guess that makes ———."

immoral – as in, "Just because he doesn't kiss a girl on the first date you think this makes ———."

impact – as in, "The train leaves in twenty minutes so you'd better get ———."

impale – as in, "I think that it was the fear of being found out that was making ———."

impart – as in, "Just because he's dating you doesn't make ——— of the family."

impassible–as in, "If we groomed him for two days we couldn't make ———."

impasse – as in, "Stand aside and let ———."

impassion – as in, "Once in the middle of the night I thought I saw ——— by."

impatible – as in, "I think that it's the baby's cuddliness that makes ———."

impatient – as in, "I don't think that giving in to him will make ———."

impeccable – as in, "I can't believe that the new feed we gave the rooster would make ———."

impenitent – as in, "It was the Saint's great life of austerity which made ———."

imperfect – as in, "He thinks that taking that course in human behavior has made ———."

impermanent – as in, "All right, Daughter, Mert can stay here temporarily, but I don't want to see ———."

impetus – as in, "If the cat were a human, and we were cats, we'd have to let ———."

impious – as in, "I believe that it was his life of crime which has now made ———."

implead – as in, "I don't care if he does say that he wants to marry me now, Mother. I want to see ———."

implied–as in, "No, don't scare him off. I want to see ——— with absolutely everything he wants."

implunge – as in, "No, he likes the water usually. You'll probably see ——— right in!"

import – as in, "No, the minister never drinks, so don't even serve ———."

impose – as in, "Yeah, just point the camera at him and you'll see ———."

impotent – as in, "It is his immense power rather than his wealth which make ——— as an enemy."

impregnate – as in, "I can only believe that he suffered a temporary loss of sanity, which made ——— the maid."

IMPRESS

impress – as in, "Take these pants back to the tailor and make —— them again."

improve – as in, "You'll have to make —— that before I'll be satisfied."

imprudent – as in, "It is his poverty-stricken background which makes —— now."

impure – as in, "Yes, my son, it was the Saint's constant dedication to God which made ——."

inalienable – to be in conformity with creatures from another planet.

inanity – as in, "We had a shower for the baby at the —— the next day."

inapt – to be inside an apartment. (shortened form)

inattention – as in, "Yes, tell your mother that we'll be living ——."

inboard – what you get along with your rented bed.

inbred – as in, "No, I don't work in the pie section of the bakery. I'm ——."

Inca – part of a song made famous by Jimmy Durante.

Incan – as in, "The cat got his tail into the —— nearly ruined the drapes when I tried to catch him."

incense – as in, "No, I used to work in dimes and quarters, but now the bank prefers me to work in nickels and ——."

incept – as in, "Y'all can come —— you'll have to leave by 4:00!"

incest – as in, "So then the guy at the —— to me, 'Pack your bags and get out!'"

incise – as in, "You should be able to make the team since you're larger than most of the boys ——."

incite – a place to build an inn.

inclose – as in, "She looks better when you get ——."

incoming – as in, "How is your work at the ——— along?"

incompatible – a good-looking lady who works in communications.

inconvertible – as in, "Chief say, 'Did you see wife ——— with medicine man?'"

incredible – as in, "We'll have to improve both our service and our advertising to make the ——— again."

incumbent – as in, "I used to make a straight salary, but now they've got my ———."

indecent – as in, "It's about time you started living ——— quarters!"

indeed – as in, "He was every inch a warrior, in truth and———." Also the title to an inn.

indefatigable – as in, "The picador thrust his lance ———."

indefinite – as in, "Well, my girl, you are ——— trouble."

indelible – a male bovine animal in a delicatessen.

indenture – to be within false teeth.

independent – as in, "If you look carefully at de Queen's necklace you will see de ruby ———."

India – as in, "There is certainly a chill ——— air."

indifferent – as in, "Well, the truth is, Mother, John and I haven't actually been living ——— apartments."

indigent – as in, "And den de witch doctor stuck a spear———."

indigo – as in, "Where did the man from ———?"

indispose – as in, "I think dat de lady look better, Sir, -———."

indoctrinate – to teach Nathan to be a doctor.

Indonesian – a person who won't go outside.

indoor baseball – a baseball stuck in a door.

induct – as in, "We saw the plane coming and everyone at the ———."

inefficiency – as in, "Yes, that might taste good. Why don't we stuff it ———."

inertial – as in, "Yes, doctor, if she finds out that we planted a transmitting device ——— flip!"

infallible – as in, "I don't know how it happened, but we were excavating under the barn when the floor gave way and———."

infamy – as in, "Oh, I just think that the teacher has it ———."

infantile – an extremely young piece of flat, kiln-fired clay.

infantry – an extremely young tree.

infect – as in, "———, I'm sure that it was, now that I think about it."

infelicity – as in, "There was always something rather wild———."

infer – as in, "So you're one of the new cons, eh? How long are ya ———?"

inferior – one who ferrys people to and from the inn.

inferno – as in, "And then after all that the coach sent me——— reason."

infest – as in, "You've been running around ——— company, haven't you?"

infield – as in, "Come quick, Bwana. Big bird come land ———."

infinity – a hot drink, brewed in Finland.

inflate – as in, "I love to watch the wild geese ———."

inflex – as in, "The paint on your car is coming off ———."

influenza – as in, "All of us ducks were having a wonderful time sitting around the pond when——— and ruined everything."

inform – keeping in shape by running around the inn.

informer – as in, "Call Nellie and ——— that we will no longer extend her credit at this establishment."

infrared – as in, "How long are ya ———?"

ingenious–as in, "Okay, I admit that it's clever, but you'd better get back to the ———."

ingest – as in, "You don't have to blow your stack! I only said it ———."

ingot – as in, "That was a nice write-up that the ———."

ingrain – as in, "Yes, I made some money off of hog futures, but I did much better ———."

ingrate – as in, "You must have been ——— shape."

inhabit – a riding costume worn around the inn.

inhale – as in, "I've been stuck in snow many times, but never ———."

inherit – as in, "A quart of beer doesn't phase me a bit but ——— becomes a demon!"

inheritance – to come into possession of some tiny red or black insects of the genus Formica.

inhuman – as in, "There is a certain quality ——— beings which makes them rotten to be around!"

injure–as in, "Say, wasn't that the sheriff I seen ———house?"

ink – an abbreviation for a corporation.

inkling – a small ink.

inkwell – as in, "Well, the baby didn't mess with the paint, but she certainly got into the ———."

inlaid – to have made love at the inn.

inland – as in, "Yes, I made most of my money ———."

inlaw–as in, "He was a good cop, but he was even better———."

innate – as in, "There's just something that's no good ——— I guess."

inner – as in, "I don't know what's got ———."

inning – traveling from inn to inn.

innkeeper – as in, "When she gets ——— there until I arrive."

innocence – as in, "——— must this be construed as giving a license to those who would use it erroneously?"

inquest – as in, "I am ——— of my fortune."

inquire – as in, "She never used to sing that badly ———."

inscribe – as in, "The King sent me to fetch you, are you ———?"

insect – as in, "Zen has become rather an ——— lately."

inset – as in, "This type of TV has become really an ———."

insinuate – as in, "Shame on you, my boy. ——— the host and you're not even Catholic!"

insist – one of those type of growths which have become popular of late.

inspector – as in, "The 'Headless Horseman' has become an ———."

inspire – one who spies on inns.

instable – where you keep the horses for the inn.

instep – as in, "You'd better keep ——— there McGooligan."

insulate – as in, "Listen, Daughter, you tell that young man that I don't want you to be getting ———."

insurance – as in, "Yes, our company has insured nearly everything. We've insured lemmings against jumping off cliffs. We've insured boll weevils against cotton. But nobody will ———."

integrate – as in, "This is going to be a wonderful year. I just feel that I'm going to get ——— things this year."

intemperance – as in, "Yes, with the proper mixture or treatment almost anything can be brought to a hardened condition. Why those entomologists down at the ———."

intend – bartender at the inn.

intense – as in, "The Smiths sold their home because they said that they wanted to be closer to nature, and now they're living ———."

interact – the juggler who comes on between your act and the main attraction.

intercede – as in, "And the Lord said, I shall make woman ——— shall populate the earth."

intercepter – a staff which the King holds in between Queens.

interchange – as in, "Here at the temple of Shurley, all who ——— their ways."

intercom – a member of the Politburo.

intercourse – making love on the fairway.

interdict – as Eisenhower said to his Vice President, "Please knock before you ———."

interfere – as in, "First, my son, there will come doubt, then despair, then ———."

interim – as in, "Don't worry about Felix getting sick. No self-respecting germ would ———."

interlock – something you eat between the cream cheese and the bagels.

interloper – a wolf who runs in the middle of the pack.

interlude – something obscene which comes in between pictures.

intermarry – something said by Joseph upon hearing a knock upon the door.

intermission – as in, "Chief say, do not attack yet. It bad medicine to ——— when great bell is ringing!"

intern – as in, "Please take a number and you will all be served ———."

interpolate – as in, "Posie is the fastest filly in the stables, but she's young yet. We don't want to race her too soon. On the other hand, we don't want to ———."

interracial – an event which occurs between heats.

interrogate – as in, "Let it be known, young Sirs, that you should never ——— without knocking first."

interval – as in, "When we left Prince Valiant yesterday, the Queen was just saying, 'You'll never be able to ———.'"

intestate – commerce which takes place between states.

intestine – as in, "Well Doctor, ——— this vaccine I have discovered that although it does not cure the common cold, it does prevent warts!"

intimacy – as in, "Yes, Sir, I'll get ——— chest and find some proper clothes for the young lady."

intolerable – means that everyone around you is taller than you.

intractable – to be unable to ride upon a tractor.

intromittent – to throw in your mittens.

intrude – as in, "We are with you in honor and ———."

intuition – as in, "Shay, you musht be drunk. Don't you know that if the ashtronauts get off coursh they could fall ———."

inundate – as in, "I don't want to go out with her. I'd rather stay ——— her sister tomorrow night."

inure – as in, "There is a wild look ——— eyes."

inveil – as in, "We used to go skiing ——— Colorado."

invent – as in, "Shame on you, Sir. Rather than break ——— your wrath upon me."

inventor – as in, "Chief say white man have mouse ——— maybe bee in bonnet."

inverse – as in, "This character was made popular ———."

inversion – as in, "Actually this is the modern or ———— of the tale."

invertebrate–to turn a woman's interwoven hair upside down.

invest – as in, "If money is not in pocket of coat, perhaps ————."

inveterate – a veteran who has the inside track.

inviolable – to be within a violin.

invoice – as in, "Are you ———— tonight, Maestro?"

inward – as in, "There's just something evil ———— that makes him do these awful things."

iodine – as in, "I don't care how much you say you love me. ————by myself all the time and I'm going to do it tonight too."

iota – as in, "———— large bill, which I paid, and now I'm broke."

irascible – as in, "You should never ————. He might get upset and gore you."

ire – as in, "The money gets less and less and the expenses get ————."

iris – as in, "And with that ———— my case, your Honor."

Irish – as in, "———— that you would stop bothering me."

irreligious–as in, "And then, your Honor, this———— nut begins reciting scriptures to me and beating me over the head with his Bible."

irreverend – as in, "We used to have fun around here. But that was before this ———— came along with all of his high and mighty ideas."

irrigate – as in, "I used to be able to tell when someone was coming because the gates used to squeak. Now, since I've oiled them, I can't ———— anymore."

Isabel – as in, "When we rang it the minister had a stroke and the church tower collapsed. Now, that ————!"

Isaiah – as in, "——— old bean, could you spare a fiver until payday?"

Isis – a greeting to your sister.

island – as in, "When I fly a plane I don't care where ———."

island hopping – as in, "Usually when I fly on this airline ——— mad!"

isle – as in, "——— bet that you really told him off."

isolate – as in, "——— that I don't think I'll ever get home."

Israel – as in, "——— Gringo? Or was it Fred."

Israelite – as in, "Thank you, but I can carry it because it ———."

issue – as in, "——— is or ——— ain't my baby?"

isthmus – as in, "I know you like living out here, but ——— make you very lonely at times."

Italian – as in, "——— you for the last time, go wash your face."

itch – as in, "——— certainly been a long time since we've seen each other."

item – as in, "If they were only having fun with him then why did Bob———."

I've – what bees live in. (Cockney)

ivy vine – a climbing vine which grows around bottles of intravenous fluids."

j

jacket – as in, "If you really want to work on this car why don't we ——— up?"

Jacobean – as in, "Tell me, Myrtle, is ———a good husband, or does he still take to drinking and have those fits?"

Jacobite – as in, "I've got to ask you, Martha, since I've seen all those marks on your neck, does ———?"

Jacob's ladder – as in, "When he was a young man he was extremely moral, but in ——— days he became a dirty old man."

jaded – to be overstocked with jade.

jaguar – as in, "If he was locked in the church, how could he have gone on a ——— there wasn't any booze?"

jail – as in, "If you mess up again ——— tell the boss, and he'll fire you."

Jane – what an anchor is attached to.

janitor – as in, "I'm telling you ——— my dress completely off of me."

January – as in, "Say ——— kin to the Hodgsons down the road?"

Japan – as in, "Tell us, Uncle Mort, how did ——— for gold in Alaska?"

jar – as in, "Did you see the lace on the badge ——— new Sheriff is wearing?"

jargon – as in, "We haven't eaten any pickles for months, so where on earth has the last ———?"

Jason – as in, "Oh no, he's ——— Fred."

jaundice – as in, "Were you a Christian before you ———?"

jaunty – one who makes many trips to the john.

jawbreaker – brass knuckles.

Jeremiah – as in, "I'm sorry, but you can't sit here. This is the ——— great grandfather."

jerkin – as in, "You're not really gonna let that ——— are you?"

Jersey – as in, "Did ——— the build on that broad."

jest – as in, "I'd ——— like to settle down somewhere and stop all of this running around."

jettison – as in, "Yes, but the old man is very strange. He refused to ride on the ———— is flying."

jetty – as in, "Did you see the ———— bought for his own private use?"

Jew – as in, "Did ———— phone me at 3:00 a.m. this morning?"

Jezebel – as in, "Don't be scared, it's ———— ringing in the church tower."

jitney – a malfunction of the large joint between the ankle and thigh.

jockstrap – a leather thong once used to beat losing riders after a race.

jodhpurs – as in, "No, he doesn't do as much as some cats, but ———— a lot."

John – a toilet.

joiner – as in, "If you can't fight her, ————."

joint account – a special savings plan open to bars and cocktail lounges. Also, in Old English, to hit a count with a leg of lamb.

joint coupling – a menage-a-quatre.

jointer – a person who frequents bars.

joint stock – a device which can punish two people at the same time.

joist – as in the old hymn, "———— a closer walk with Thee."

joke – as in, "If you won't take me out I'm sure that————can."

Jonah – as in, "———— Arc."

journey – as in, "Did ———— ever get back to normal after I kicked it?"

joust – as in, "Please give me ———— one more chance."

joyful – how she feels after Thanksgiving.

Judah – as in, "Before I could reach the dog he ——— big hole in little Sidney's pants."

Judas – as in, "I remember a past life when I, along with my family, was thrown to a lion, and he ——— up."

judgment – as in, "I wonder what the ——— when he said you were a menace?"

Juggernaut – referring to drinking, as in, "To ——— to jug."

juggle – as in, "If they send me up the ——— drive me crazy."

juggling – drinking from a jug.

jugular – one who drinks from a jug.

juice – people descended from the ancient Hebrews.

Julian – as in, "Did ——— on my bell for about ten minutes last night?"

Juliet – as in, "You should see the huge dinner that ———."

July – as in, "I know that you didn't mean to, but why did ——— about it?"

jumper – as in, "When she comes around the corner let's ———."

junction – as in, "Shay, you'd better get rid of that ———."

juncture – as in, "I see that you finally ——— old car!"

June beetle – member of a well-known rock group who only lasted one month.

June bug – as in, "She's very insistent, so don't let ——— you too much."

junior – as in, "Oh, I didn't know; is ——— daughter?"

juniper – as in, "I know that she doesn't like Mary Lou, but why did ——— with the pliers?"

junket – as in, "You've been driving that old heap for twenty years. Why don't you ——— and get something decent to drive?"

Juno – as in, "Did —— that your wife was seeing another man?"

Jupiter – as in, "I know that she's a good tennis player, but would —— against a real pro?"

Jurassic – one who has been on a lot of juries."

jurisdiction – to speak like a juror.

jury box – as in, "And then sometimes, to give them a little exercise, we take them all down to the gym and let the ——."

jury-rigged – one that has been bought off.

justice – as in, "It —— not going to take very long to get there."

jute – meaning, "Go ahead and fire the gun." (Mexican)

juvenile – teenagers on a major Egyptian river.

k

kaiser – as in, "We have beautiful sunsets too, just take a look at that s——."

Kama – a type of punctuation.

Kanaka – as in, "Is that Dick—— on your door?"

kangaroo rat–a device used to embellish a kangaroo's coiffure."

karma – as in, "Why did Daddy wreck the ——?"

Kashmir–as in, "And as for—— money will never impress me!"

katydid – as in, "Jane may be fun on a date, but I bet she'll never do what ——."

kazoo – as in, "I'm not going to tell you —— will tell everyone."

keel – as in, "Tell my Jimmy I gonna —— heem."

keelhaul – "We gonna —— those rebels with their own weapons."

keeper – as in, "How you gonna ——— down on the farm?"

kennel – as in, "Don't worry, ——— be here with you."

keno – an expression of approval.

Kentucky – used to chase girls down at the high school.

kerchief – as in, "She's always been a good worker here at the bureau, so why would she sock ———?"

kernel – an army officer.

kerosene – as in, "Of course I'm shouting! I don't ——— might do us both good!"

kettle – as in, "I'm telling you that he's rotten. That ——— come to no good. Mark my words."

keyboard – as in, "I've never seen a locksmith take so long. Isn't that ——— yet?"

keyhole – as in, "Don't break it! I want my ———."

keystone – used by ancient singers to get the pitch. They would drop a rock upon a larger one and take their note from the sound produced.

khan – as in, "If I ——— you ——— too."

kickback – used in football, as in, "I sure wish that we had that ———."

kickoff – as in, "I don't think there will be time to get the ———."

kid gloves – what you put on children in the winter.

kidnap – what you give your child in the middle of the day.

kidney – the main joint of your child's leg, between the ankle and the thigh.

kidney bean – as in, "Hi, Joe, how's your ———?"

kiln – as in, "I'm not ——— this keg all by myself!"

kilo – a very low key.

kilocycle – as in, "Yes, he was really weird. He used to go around shooting at Hondas, trying to ———."

kilowatt-hour – as in, "And if we stoop to ———— society is coming to."

kilter – as in, "Their physical relationship became so strenous that it finally ————."

Kimono – as in, "Did I hear ———— was that just the wind sighing?" Also a name for a dragon.

kindle – as in, "I hardly ever see my relatives because I find most of my ————."

kindly – as in, "Don't treat Gloria like a tramp. She's not that ————."

kindred – as in, "He is so obnoxious that all of his ———— to see him coming."

king crab – as in, "I know he didn't like the feast, but why would the ———— about the dancing girls?"

kingdom – as in, "The Queen refuses to come out of her bed chamber. She says that she finds the ————."

kingfish – as in, "Yes, our monarch is quite an outdoorsman. In fact I've often seen the ————."

Kingfisher – as in, "Unfortunately, the Queen is rather stupid, and many mornings I've seen the ———— out of the moat."

King Lear – as in, "I just saw the ———— at one of the dancing girls."

kingly – as in, "No no, you mustn't throw rocks at the ————." Also a title sometimes applied to Liberace.

kingpin – a fastener used by monarchs.

kinship – as in, "I'd sure hate to see our ———— Myrtle out here for the summer."

kipper – as in, "Okay, but I can't ———— here for very long."

kirsch – as in, "Of ———— she does."

kismet – as in, "He discovered that his ———— with a strong response from her."

kingfisher

kitchenette – to eat a kitchen.

kitten – as in, "No, I made it from this ——— that's why I can't understand it coming out like this."

kittenish – to like young cats.

kiwi – a small key.

knapsack – a sleeping bag.

knarl – a warning sound, made by a harelipped dog.

knead – as in, "Don't leave me, Harry, I ——— you."

kneecap – a hat worn upon the knee.

kneel – a man's name.

knell – a woman's name.

knickknack – as in, "Yes, Nicholas has a certain way with women. It's sort of a ———."

knighthood – a criminal at King Arthur's court.

knightly – as in, "I used to see her ———."

knit – as in, "Don't spend your time ——— picking."

knock-knee – to rap with the knuckles upon someone's kneecap.

knotty – as in, "If ——— may find himself all alone."

kodiak bear – a picture-taking ursine.

kookaburra – as in, "I knew that old prospector was hungry, but why would he ———?"

Koran – as in, "When I was in the Marines the whole ——— everytime the general appeared."

kosher – as in, "I'm leaving now. ——— welcome to stay as long as you like."

kumquat – as in, "Well, we've ——— a ways since this morning."

Kurd – as in, "It just a——— to me that we left little Alice locked in the bathroom."

134

I

label – French name for what the Hunchback rang.

labor – French name for a male pig.

Labor Day – nine months after Father's Day.

laborious – French device for tunnelling.

labor of love – having a child.

labor party – a female.

labor saving – contraceptives.

labor union – something which by all rights should be physically impossible.

lace – as in, "It doesn't do anything, it just —— there."

lacerate – as in, "Oh, poor, itty, bitty lion. Her's a bad girl, yes. What happened to that —— huh?"

lacework – as in, "No matter how plain the rest of your dress is, you're never going to make that ——."

lackey – as in, "It wasn't so much that he was in —— just liked to steal things."

lacquer – as in, "I just don't —— hanging around my husband."

lacrosse – name for that which you find on top of a church steeple. (French)

lactose – as in, "Oh yes, Sir, I —— very much!"

lacy – as in, "I feel very —— this afternoon."

ladder – as in, "What ever happened to that —— sister was running around with?"

laddie – a short ladder. (Scottish)

lade – as in, "She just —— there sneering at me."

ladle – as in, "After the hens —— the eggs they could, we cooked a twenty pound omelet."

lady bug – an eavesdropping device for females.

ladylike – describes a female impersonator.

ladyship – as in, "But why did the —— her husband off to the Colonies if she was a nymphomaniac?"

lag – as in, "Stop hangin' onto my —— gal. I got to get outta here."

lager beer – a brew which is sold only to lumberjacks.

lagoon – French word for a thug.

lair – as in, "Bring in that sick cow and we'll —— right here next to the TV."

laissez faire – as in, "It was much better last year. This is really a ——."

lama – Spanish for the mother.

lamb – a quick flight.

lambaste – a sauce which is poured over the lamb from time to time.

lambent – a crooked lamb.

lambskin – the relatives of the lamb.

laminate – as in, "We were on the —— wanted to go back for his teddy bear. That's how we got caught."

lance – as in, "Why don't we just throw it and see where it ——?"

Lancelot – a pilot who can't stay in the air.

lancer – as in, "Buckle your seat belt, we're about to ——."

landau – as in, "I know we've got to land, but ——?"

land crab – when someone tries to get control of a large piece of land.

landlord – as in, "If that was my —— how I'd want to sell out."

landmark – as in, "Where did you ———?"

land tax – short, sharply pointed nails which are placed so as to pierce the feet of trespassers.

lantern – as in, "With a strong enough earthquake on this island you could possibly see the ——— completely upside down."

Laplander – that which suddenly lands in your lap. Also a girl who sits in the laps of all the males at a party.

lapping – sitting on laps.

lapse – that which you sit on.

lariat – as in, "I found George and Fred, but where is ———?"

larynx – a wildcat.

lasso – as in, "Did you find the ——— ran off with your son?"

latent – something put up by a tardy camper.

lateral – as in, "No, I think that this ——— reach up there okay."

latest – a French test.

lathe – as in, "I'm thorry, but she jutht ——— there and doth nothing."

Latin – a cross between linen and satin.

Latinize – what Spanish girls have two of.

Latin Quarter – one fourth of a Latin Dollar.

latter – something to climb to reach a high shelf.

lattice – as in, "This ——— really very bright, Father."

launch – a meal to eat in the middle of the day.

launder – as in, "I ——— my tennis racket and she never brought it back."

lavender – as in, "No, I ——— next house down."

lay of the land – a prostitute who really gets around.

lazy – as in, "All right, M'seur. ——— sword down very carefully!" (French)

leaf spring – as in, "From whence did this ———?"

lean-to – as in, "No, you look pretty ——— me."

lease – that which belongs to Lee.

leaven – as in, "Now we're really ———."

leaving – a tree losing its foliage.

lecher – as in, "Well, my boy, just ——— conscience be your guide!"

lecithin – as in, "If you keep on eating those pies you're going to be ——— than you would like."

ledger – as in, "Yes, Sir Boswald, I'm afraid that the rowing team has ——— daughter into a life of sin."

leech – to extend the arm, or to stretch out toward something. (Chinese)

legacy – as in, "Okay, Buster, you'd better let go of my ———."

legate – as in, "If you hadn't been trying to kick the tiger, you wouldn't have got your ———."

legend – as in, "I don't care if we are the first people to scale Mount Stupid. My immediate concern is where does this ———?"

Leghorn – a device which, when strapped to the leg, is used to sound a warning when walking in traffic.

legion – as in, "That kid is going to ——— right into the poor house."

legislator – as in, "Either Mr. ——— we're early."

legitimate–living with a person to whom you are legally married.

leg-of-mutton – as in, "Whatta ya mean these people don't eat dogs! I just saw a ——— the butcher's counter."

legume – a shallow body of water, separated from the sea by low banks.

Leghorn

leisure – as in, "You can't just walk out on him. After all, ——— husband."

lemming – a yellow citrus fruit.

lemonade – a society which furnishes assistance and comfort to lemmings.

lemur – as in, "If you go in there ——— nuts!"

lenient – as in, "Stand back. The building is ——— this way."

lentil – as in, "I can't cut the grass, the lawnmower is ——— next Tuesday."

leprosy – a body of water surrounding the Greek Island of Lepros.

Lesbian – as in, "Why is ——— so nice to me today?"

lethal – as in, "Thith ——— keep the property tied up for yearth."

letter – as in, "If she wants to mess around with other guys, ———."

letterhead – as in, "She must ———, not her heart be her guide."

lettuce – as in, "Come, my Darling, ——— be friends."

levee – what the Government uses to extract money from you.

levity – a feeling of warm affection for that upon which you place your golf ball.

lewd – as in, "Mother, I never thought that ——— try to do that on our very first date!"

lexicon – as in, "Yes, I use this dog to spot convicts. He bites cops but he always ———."

liable – to speak an untruth to a male bovine animal.

liason – as in, "I can not tell a ——— is better than no child at all!"

libel – as Bat Masterson once said to Miss Starr, "Why did you ———?"

liberal – as in, "Yep, she's a women's ——— the way."

liberate – as in, "And this is the poisoned pizza which that women's ——— just before she died."

liberty – a late afternoon snack served to proponents of women's liberation.

library – as in, "It doesn't ——— far from here."

license – to be smart enough to know when not to tell the truth.

lichen – a cross between the library and the kitchen.

licorice – title for the office worker who seals envelopes.

lieu – a man's name.

life-buoy – as in, "Not on your ———!"

ligature – as in, "Why, Jon, you and Freda are all covered with hay, just ———selves."

lighten – as in, "There on the battlefield ——— of the nation's finest."

light-headed – a moth.

light-hearted – one of Doctor Christian Barnard's donors.

lightning bug – one who is obsessed with electrical storms.

light-year – as in, "Here, take this candle to ——— way."

lignite – a perfect evening for observing the supporting members of the female body.

likely – as in, "I really go for Fred, but I don't ———."

likeness – the name of a monster, found in Scotland.

lilliputian – used to be librarian down at the high school.

lily-livered – a sad condition caused by eating plants of the genus lilium.

lily-white – Snow White's sister.

limit – to cut the branches off a tree.

limited – as in, "I don't care how nice you say you'll be from now on. I'm up to my ———."

limp – as in, "Now we're really out on a ———."

limpet – an unconscious cat or dog.

line – a large member of the cat family, indigenous to Africa.

linear – as in, "Just ——— and I will tell of the strange misfortunes which befell our hero and heroine."

lineman – one who tells women stories designed to promote relationships.

linger – as in, "He is a dead ——— for Jack." (Chinese)

lint – a period of forty days preceding Easter.

lion – as in, "The D.A. thinks that you are ———, Mc Ginty."

lip service – a kissing booth.

liqueur – as in, "She may be taller, but I can ——— any day."

list – as in, "——— we forget."

listen – as in, "Take this ——— go to the store."

listless – when you forgot your list.

litany – as in, "Now, students, standing in this relaxed posture, slowly bend one leg and ——— touch the ground."

literal – as in, "I thought that you were going to clean up all of this ———."

literature – as in, "You can throw things on the table; you can throw things on the couch; but you'd better not ———."

lithe – as in, "Thath all a pack of ———."

litmus – as in, "The lamp, when ——— not be allowed to burn with too high a flame."

livelihood – a vigorous or active crook.

livery – a dormitory.

livid – as in, "I have ——— in this house for years."

load – as in, "In the barn one of the cattle ———."

loan – as in, "I will meet you at dawn, and come a————."

lobby – small insect which pollinates and gathers honey. (Spanish)

lobster – a cricket player who throws slow underhand balls.

local – something not very high in calories. Also a greeting to Calvin.

locker – as in, "If she tries to escape ———— up."

locks – kosher salmon.

locomotive – a crazy reason.

loco weed – as in, "If they hadn't been so ———— have felt more secure."

lode – as in, "That old miner is carrying quite a ————."

lodgement – as in, "All the world wonders what Ambassador ———— by that statement."

lofty – warehouses with upper stories.

loganberry – as in, "Is ———— serious about moving in here with you?"

logbook – a record kept by the primitive tribes of Guatemala, which was written upon sections of tree trunk.

loggerhead – a toilet for those who harvest trees.

loggy – a small log.

loin – to acquire knowledge, experience or skill.

loiter – as in, "———— I found out that it wasn't true."

lollipop – as in, "You'd better let go of my ———— or I'll scream!" (Cockney)

lonely – as in, "How long have you been a ————?"

longbow – a tall hobo.

longshoreman – as in, "I find this bottle washed up ————."

longsuffering – as in, "I kept on mowing the ———— all the while."

loom – part of the space within a house or building, separated by walls or partitions from the rest. (Chinese)

loose – as in, "If we ———— this game, you're through!"

loosen – as in, "We could ———— still be number one this year."

loot – as in, "We do not encourage this type of ———— conduct at our school."

loquat – as in, "Hey, ———— Grandma brought us."

lord – from the popular Irish song, "Clancy ———— the boom."

lore – as in, "I'm going down to the ———— forty this morning."

lorry – a girl's name.

loss – rules and regulations which society passes to protect and govern itself.

lottery – as in, "This investment should bring you a ———— turn."

lotus – as in, "After this the terrorists proceeded to ———— all on a bus."

loud – as in, "Such conduct is not a————."

loudspeaker – what you find at community dinners.

louse – as in, "You will get all the protection that the law a————."

lovely – as in, "I ————, but he says that I am a pest."

low – a greeting.

lowborn – this is what happens when you book your wife into a maternity ward that's below ground level.

lowboy – a greeting to a male.

lowbred – very little money.

lowbrow – a disfiguration caused by wearing hats which are too heavy.

lowering – as in, "She has a wart on her middle finger. It's just be————."

lowland – what you experience when you bring a plane into Death Valley.

loyal – as in, "The British ——— Family." (Chinese)

lozenge – as in, "In this society most of our ——— upon the will of the majority."

lubber – a person who is enamored of members of the opposite sex.

lubberly – an expression used in "My Fair Lady," as in, "Oh, wouldn't it be ———."

lubricate – used to be a custodian down at the high school.

lucid – used to be a Spanish Commander in Chief.

Lucifer – as in, "All right, my boy, you'd better let ———."

luck – as in, "Just ——— at the mess you've caused!"

lucky – as in, "We're in ——— hasn't left yet."

lucre – as in, "We're going out to the ranch and ——— over."

luff – a feeling of warmth and affection toward someone.

luke – as in, "Now just ——— what you've done to me."

lumber – as in, "I don't know whether the voice I heard was ——— Abner."

lumberjack – as in, "You'd better take your hands off of that ———."

lumen – as in, "There is a dark shape ——— up ahead."

luminate – as in, "I know you are familiar with textile plants, but do you know how to operate this ———?"

lunacy – to be enamored of a loon.

lunatic – an even trade, one for one, a loon for a tick and visa versa.

lunch – as in, "He made a sudden ——— for me but I was able to avoid him."

luncheon – as in, "I don't want to have —— the roof."

lunge – a light meal between breakfast and dinner.

lupine – as in, "We were —— tinsel around the tree when our Christmas Carp suddenly exploded in the oven."

lurid – as in, "With candy and sweets he —— her into his miserable hovel."

luscious – as in, "If he opened the valve he might half—— down the drain."

luster – as in, "I followed the lady to the inn, Mi'Lord, where I —— in the dark."

lute – booty, spoils, or plunder.

Lutheran – one who plunders, or pillages.

luxuriant – pertains to relaxing in a hot tub with many suds of a well known soap.

lycanthrope – as in, "—— a good deal of material clogging your pipes. It can also wreck them."

lyceum – as in, "Why did you ——?"

lye – an untruth.

lymph – a girl who is unable to control her sexual appetite.

lynx – where you play golf.

lyonnaise – as in, "I'm not —— really the one who did it!"

lyre – one who tells lyes.

lyric – as in, "You shouldn't have given that girl such a ——."

macabre – as in, "I don't give a damn about the corn, I just want ——."

macaque – as in, "I hope that the authorities who confiscated our fighting birds give me back ———."

macaroon – as in, "If you keep hacking away at that dress Martha, you're gonna ——— out of it."

Macassar – as in, "Well, Doc, are you gonna remove ——— do I have to wear it for another month?"

macaw – as in, "Miss Jones, will you transfer ——— from line five?"

mace – as in, "Yes, it's been very chilly. Most ——— we have much warmer weather."

machinate – as in, "If the elevator fails while he's working under it, the car could very easily ———."

machine – the Bishop's mother.

mackerel – a waterproof cloak or coat for use in wet weather.

madcap – headgear used in asylums to distinguish patients from staff.

made – female household servant.

made-up – as in, "Which one of your nephews knocked the ———?"

madonna – as in, "If I can't get Sally to live with me, I'll just stay with ———."

maelstrom – a place in the post office where your letters go 'round and 'round and are never delivered.

magnet – a woven construction of knotted cords designed to catch magazines.

magneto – a really great magazine.

magnificent – a splendidly impressive penny.

magnolia – a greater or improved type of linoleum.

magpie – a dessert made from old, shredded magazines.

mah-jong – famous Chinese madam.

maelstrom

mahogany – as in, "Bring me the phone, Bertha. I want to call the vet and see is ——— better this morning."

maiden – as in, "This product was ——— Japan."

maiden-head – a toilet in a girls' school.

maidenly – as in, "Shame on you! Take your hands off that ———."

maim – someone's Auntie.

mainsail – what the stores have just preceding tax time.

maitre d'hotel – as in, "She's never serious about anything so I ——— clown."

major – as in, "We're practically related. After all, I——— sister!"

major general – as in, "You have lost face. Not only have we beaten you in battle, but we have ——— the laughing stock of all Europe!"

makeshift – from four to midnight in a brothel when the real professionals are on duty.

malachite – as in, "I don't mind Matthew having a top, but why on earth did you buy ———?"

malaria – as in, "I'm gonna rope this calf. Where's ———at?"

Malayan – as in, "The other hens don't produce much, but this one here is ——— hen."

malemute – as in, "Yes, he was so frightened of girls that on his very first date he lost his voice. And that's what made———."

malformed – as in, "This is the band that ——— while he was in the army."

malice – as in, "Don't go out with him, Judy. ——— oversexed and undernourished!"

malicious – as in, "In fact, ——— a lousy date all around!"

malign – as in, "May lightening strike me dead if I'm ———."

Maltese – a strip done by a girl who had too many malted milks.

149

mammoth – as in, "A —— do what he hath to!"

management – as in, "Women, who are past the time of their lives in which they were dating may remember regretfully what the ——."

manager – as in, "She's pretty wild but I can ——."

manakin – as in, "Thank goodness for the battle of the sexes. That's what gives a ——."

manatee – as in, "He's so stingy with his golf equipment that he wouldn't even give a ——."

Manchu – as in, "Boy, he must really have been hungry! Look at that ——."

mandamus – as in, "I know he doesn't approve of us, but why would the ——?"

mandarin duck – as in, "Wait 'til those peasants start throwing things. That's when you'll see the ——."

mandate – what you get when you call one of those numbers on the walls of the men's room, and it turns out to be a guy.

mandatory – as in, "The Whigs are all right, but —— government is terrible!"

mandrill – as in, "I've worked in the oil fields for over forty years and I've never seen anything like this. Just look at that ——."

mane – a state in New England.

man-eater – as in, "I knew he didn't like the horse, but I never thought that I'd see the ——."

manful – as in, "I've never had such good cooking. You really know how to get a ——."

mange – a small manger.

mangle – a cross between a mop and a bangle.

mango – as in, "Don't fret, Daughter, just let the ——."

mangrove – a clump of trees in which male humans live.

mangy – a person who lives in the Northeastern-most state of the U.S.

mania – as in, "——— young girl has learned this lesson too late."

manicure – as in, "Why don't you try the witch doctor? You don't care how it happens, ——— is what you're after!'"

manifold – as in, "I see that you don't know nothin' about doin' laundry. ——— in the right place will make it a lot easier to put these clothes away!"

manipulate – as in, "She may not catch on to you early, but I'll bet we see ———."

mankind – as in, "It is a genuine concern for others which makes a ———."

manna – as in, "I'm a ——— very few words!"

manner – as in, "Since he took that trip to Sweden, I don't know whether he is a ——— not!"

mannerly – as in, "He doesn't know just who attacked him. It could have been a ——— dressed up like one."

mannish – as in, "Thish ——— accoshting me offisher."

man-of-war – Attila the Hun.

manor – as in, "Well, daughter, either go out with this ——— prepare yourself for becoming an old maid."

manse – as in, "This ——— a menace to the whole community!"

mansion – as in, "It is the little peculiarities of some women which sometimes makes a ——— their company!"

mantel – as in, "I saw that ——— the sheriff on you."

mantelpiece – an Old English expression which came from making love over a fireplace.

mantis – as in, "'Tis not a ——— a boy who standeth here."

manual – as in, "The king says that he is the ——— soon marry."

manumit – as in, "Isn't he the ——— at the party last Saturday?"

manure – as in, "He is the ——— father wants you to marry."

many-headed – as in, "After a meal of raw frogs and licorice soup, ——— for the restrooms to relieve themselves of their dinners."

manzanita – as in, "You couldn't be more wrong! This ——— guy!"

maple – as in, "The trials of life ——— you back, but struggle ever onward."

maraschino – as in, "I don't know how, but that ——— when the stallion is around."

marathon – as in, "Ever since you read *All You Ever Wanted To Know About Sex* to the animals, there's been something queer going on around this ranch. I just came from the barn, and now the ——— the stallion!"

marble – character in an Agatha Christie novel.

march – a woman's name.

mare – as in, "Come ——— you cute little filly, you."

margin – as in, "Bartender, ——— all around."

Marianne – as in, "I might marry Sue, but I would certainly never ———."

marigold – as in, "She isn't interested in the man she marries. She just wants to ———."

marinate – as in, "In fact, she doesn't want to ——— until he quits living with Frances."

marionette – a veil placed over the heads of a man and woman during a wedding ceremony in the Fiji Islands. Also, the dream of many male Mickey Mouse Club viewers during the 1950s.

marital – as in, "The stallion wouldn't go near the ———."

maritime – as in, "After we unhitched her though he really gave the ———."

marjoram – as in, "I thought you were fond of that old sheep, so why did you give ———?"

market – as in, "Before we start cutting let's ——— with a pencil."

marksman – as in, "He'll never work for the Circle Bar S. He's strictly ———."

marmalade – as the baby duck said, "My ——— me!"

marquee – something overheard in a Hong Kong tailor shop. "You likee I ——— these pants here?"

marriage – as in, "I think that it was the continual stud service which made the ——— so fast."

marshal – as in, "Yep, if folks go wanderin' around out there at night why the ——— just swallow them up sometimes."

marshmallow – a large squash which grows in bogs.

martial – as in, "If you say that to her ——— slap your face."

martinet – as in, "Did you see the size of the meal that ———?"

martyr – as in, "I'm afraid that the presence of her boyfriend living in the same house ——— marriage to Fred."

mascot – as in, "Last summer I got ——— in the crotch of a big tree and couldn't get down for five days."

masculine – as in, "Let ———, do you ever fool around?"

masochism – as in, "I don't like those kind of parties. They're nothing but a ——— and fooling around!"

Mason and Dixon – used to have a dog act on the old Borscht circuit.

masonic – as in, "I don't care how good a flyer you are. ——— booms are louder than yours!"

masquerade – as in, "She gives money through the Red Cross, so as to ——— to him."

mass – as in, "This is a fine ——— that you've gotten us into!"

massacres – as in, "I never saw so many nondescript dogs in my life. They certainly are a ———."

massage – as in, "You're a nasty man, Corporal Smedley, and I'm going to go and tell ——— on you!"

massive – as in, "The boss is gonna fire ——— he catches us together here in the washroom!"

mastiff – as in, "We simply ——— we are to remain friends."

mastodon – as in, "You'll never sail that boat again! I gave the ———."

mate–as in, "I ——— a serious mistake when I hired you, Ferdley!"

matriarch – a luminous incandescence, caused by the passage of electrical current when your mother is welding.

matricide – your mother's portion of the bed.

matter – as in, "Yes, I ——— at a party at Googie's house."

mattress – a lady who makes mats.

mature – as in, "Hey, that's my ——— standing on!"

maudlin – used to be a cheerleader down at the high school.

maxim – as in, "Yes, Bwana. ——— take beaters and go into bush early this morning."

maximum – a very heavy English mother.

maybe – a small honey-producing insect which lives only during this month.

mayonnaise – as in, "According to our bylaws we can not adjourn this meeting on a yea vote, but we ———."

mayor – as in, "She ——— she may not like you. It depends on how much money you spend on her."

meadowlark – a prank pulled off in the cow pasture.

mean – as in, "——— Joe are going over to Debby's house."

meander – as in, "——— lived together for a whole term until the dean caught us."

measure – as in, "I couldn't marry you in April, John. But if it's in ——— I will!"

Mecca – as in, "This place would ——— garbage dump. Don't you ever clean house anymore?"

medallion – as in, "I'm not welcome at the castle anymore since Lord Crudly caught ——— with his daughter."

meddle – as in the title, "The American ——— Association."

medicine – a breaking of the Seventh Commandment, practiced by doctors and nurses.

megaphone – as in, "I'm tired of continuously having our phone tied up by these kids! Why don't we get ——— of her own."

megawatt – as in, "You want to give ———?"

melancholic – a croupy cough caused by eating melons.

melancholy – as the farmer said to Lassie, "You'd better not eat that ———."

melee – a horizontal association with a person of the opposite sex during the month between April and June.

mellow – as in, "I was surprised because he's always so happy. I've never seen ——— before."

melon – as in, "He is really hyped up today. What the heck is ———?"

melting pot – something attempted by subjection of marijuana to extremely high temperatures.

memento – as in, "Okay, Sheriff, I told ——— throw down their guns and come out."

menace – as in, "I has told you, daughter, that ——— simply no good!"

menial – as in, "The Queen will never see ———, no matter what the occasion!"

metronome

mention – as in, "What makes ——— the company of those who love them?"

mentor – as in, "Warden, the ——— out all the urinals and have been dropping them on us from the second floor."

menu – as in, "No, Shirley, I'm not going to end up like the rest of the ——— date!"

mercerize – blurred vision caused by sight reading too many of Johnny's old tunes.

merchandise – as in, "His daughter must agree to marry the king by midnight, otherwise the ———."

mere – as in, "Come ——— you idiot."

merrymaker – as in, "Why did ——— husband sleep in the chicken coop last night?"

messenger – as in, "I guess that since your wife went home to her mother's you've been ——— home cooked meals."

Messiah – as in, "——— continually warn you, Kunkley, not to use that sort of language when addressing your students?"

metal – as in, "I guess that you've ——— the girls by now."

metaphor – as in, "I've occasionally met some people who are pay grade two or three, and just this morning I ———."

metaphysical – as in, "Last night I ——— girl if there ever was one!"

mete – animal flesh, used for food.

meteor – as in, "I like this casserole, it's ———."

meter – as in, "Yeah, she's really beautiful. Would you like to ———?"

metric – as in, "Janet is a different person since she ———."

metronome – a mythical dwarf who inhabits metropolitan districts.

metropole – a metropolitan inhabitant of Poland.

mettle – as in, "I've told you before not to ——— in my affairs."

mezzanine – Chopin's ninth piano composition.

microbe – outer garment worn while speaking on a microphone.

microscope – as in, "I can't shoot those pesky crows if I can't see them! Which one of you kids took ——— off this rifle?"

Midas – as in, "Oh ——— your husband have another woman, dear?"

midget – as in, "There ain't no more food. ——— everything in sight!"

midnight – as in, "Oh, long she watched her beauty fade, ——— and knave she plied her trade."

midwife – the one you married between the first and third ones.

mien – as in, "——— Jack are gonna play leap-frog in the back yard."

migrate – as in, "And this is ——— big brother, Dumbo."

milligram – a telegram from her personally.

million – as in, "Hey Frank, it's ——— line two."

millwright – as in, "My boy, you'll never learn to operate this ———."

minaret – a popular dance with very small, stately steps.

mince – as in, "Gentlemen, the ——— simply are not turning out enough money anymore."

minded – as in, "Your date might not have wanted to fool around, but ———."

miniature – as in, "Hey, Mickey, ——— piece of cheese."

minimum – a small, English mother.

minister – as in, "And while she slept, strange thoughts ——— peaceful dreams."

minnow – as in, "If you're asking ——— you can't!"

microbe

minor – as in, "Did he want ——— not."

minority – a sorority of miners' wives.

Minotaur – as in, "I can't believe it. The ——— backs are turned, you run off with the TV repairman."

minuet – as one cannibal said to another, "You've had a good, productive life. Just think of all the ———."

minute hand – as in, "In about a ——— me the bomb."

miracle – as in, "A melon which ripens on the vine is a ———."

mirror – as in, "Come ——— I'll beat you up."

misadventure – as in, "I wouldn't be surprised to see that——— into some things which no respectable young lady should know about."

misappropriate – as in, "Well, ——— is not the way I would describe your actions.

misbehave – as in, "If you're going to make that ——— you'll have to do more than just talk to her."

misconception – as in, "Yes, ——— is possible at your age, but not from kissing someone."

miscount – a daughter of the nobility.

misdemean – as in, "You can come out now———old man has gone away."

misease – as in, "Well, ——— just one of those fellow who likes to hand young girls a line."

miser – as in, "Oh——— you certainly have a way with women."

misfire – as in, "If he shows up again ——— off that horse pistol and I'll come a-runnin'."

misgiving – as in, "Yes, Sister Sarah. I found this young ——— away her affections to a band of traveling musicians, out behind the barn."

misinform – as in, "I prescribe proper diet and lots of exercise to keep this young ———."

mislike – as in, "Let's see, that's three hamburgers, two cokes, and a root beer. And what would the young ———?"

mismanage – as in, "Take my advice ——— your affairs a little better and you won't have to write home for more money before the term ends."

mismate – a female officer on a merchant ship.

misnomer – as in, "Please ——— tarts. I'm about to burst."

mispronounce – as in, "No, ——— are never used in place of adjectives."

misrepresents – as in, "This, ——— a serious breech of conduct on your part."

missing link – a lost golf course.

mission – as in, "I've been ——— your kission ever since you went away!"

missionary – as in, "He's got to be the world's champeen turkey shooter! He ain't ——— one of them."

mist – as in, "Ha, ha, you ——— me!"

mistake–as in, "We ——— time to get to know each other better."

mistle-toe – an affliction which comes from having a rocket dropped upon your foot. (Prevalent at Cape Canaveral)

mite – as in, "I ——— consider it if you throw in two mules and your Honda."

mitre – as in, "Well, she ——— then again she might not."

mitre box – as in, "We are poor people, Sir, and cannot afford an expensive funeral. ——— not be made of fiber board or plastic?"

mitigate – as in, "Ich habe ein haus ———." (German)

mitten – as in, "Ich habe zwei frau, ——— kinder." (German)

mix – something belonging to Mickey.

mixer – as in, "My wife thinks she knows me well, so tonight I'm gonna ———— up by bringing my girlfriend home to dinner."

mixture – as in, "Oh, Doctor Jekyll, I ———— drink that was left over with the cat's dinner."

Mizpah – a leader of women's rights.

mizzen – as in, "What we women need is a ———— the White House."

Moabites – as in, "I'm not going to date him anymore, Mother ————."

moaning – a greeting used early in the day by Jimmy Carter.

mobilize – as in, "The Alabama Supreme Court didn't believe her story, and what's more, that sheriff down in ————."

moccasin – as in, "No, my son, such downward tendencies need to be overcome, and what's more you must never————."

model – as in, "He found Pa very exciting, but he found————."

modest – as in, "When she cleaned house did ———— in here?"

modesty – as in, "No, nothing fancy. It will just be a ————."

Mogul – as in, "I never thought that these sea birds could taste so good. Gimme ————."

Mohammedan – as in, "———— I pounded for hours and still couldn't raise anyone!"

molar – as in, "Is that animal a ———— a gopher?"

molasses – the tail ends of small burrowing animals.

mold – as in, "This here is ———— partner, Abner!"

molder – as in, "I'm gonna———— into a real pool shark one of these days!"

molest – as in, "You should never pet a ———— he bite you."

mollycoddle – as in, "You should see ———— an egg."

molten – as in, "We've caught nine moles before, and this is ———."

monastery – as in, "What kind of a ——— that he would desert us in our hour of need?"

moneylender – as in, "She would for ——— body to whomever could pay."

money-maker – as in, "Oft would the clink of ——— eyes shine brightly."

monger – as in, "Come ——— folks are due back any minute now and we're not dressed yet."

monkey – as in, "We'd better get out of here. That ——— told the Bishop that we were witches."

monk-hood – a syndicate spy in a monastery.

monogram – a singing telegram which won't play in stereo.

monologue – a book for keeping track of non-stereo recordings. Also a single section of tree trunk.

monopoly – as the Italian immigrant said, "I'm a sure gonna miss ———."

monotone – as in, "When you write to Mother, tell her that the stereo volume is working great, but tell ——— control at all."

Monroe doctrine – that which Marilyn put upon Joe during their marriage.

monsoon – as in, "We'd better find the ——— or the IRA will have him."

monster – as in, "I've never seen such a speedy chef's helper before. Just watch that ———."

monument – as in, "Father Murphy, is this not the ——— us to hire?"

moonfaced – as in, "As he uttered these words, Reverend ——— to the North and bowed three times from the waist."

163

moonlight – as in, "It has long been known that the moon is actually constructed of styrofoam, and this is what makes the ———."

Moor – as in, "Being Mayor of this town is not enough for me, I tell you. I want ——— and ——— and ———."

moorish – a sailor who doesn't want to leave the dock.

moppet – as in, "Now, you girls can just pick up the kitchen floor and ———."

moraine – as in, "The weather forecast says we're in for ———."

morale – as in, "I'm glad that you like my pickled peanut butter. Would you care for some ———?"

moralize – as in, "I can tell that she'd never do anything wrong. She has very ———."

morass – what you get when you put on too much weight.

morbid – as in, "I don't think that we are going to get this contract. I wish that we had ——— on it."

moron – as in, "His show wasn't very good yesterday, but he's ——— today."

morsel – as in, "Gentlemen, we're just not getting the product across. What we need here is ———."

mortal – as in, "If he catches you out there with Cousin Lulu, Uncle ——— skin you alive."

mortar – as in, "I don't care if you're in love with ——— not. No daughter of mine is going to run away with a dirty book salesman."

mortise – as in, "But, Mother, ——— so cute."

Mosaic – used to run the delicatessen across from the high school.

mosque – something you place over your face to keep from being recognized.

mosquito – as in, "Yes, the ski lodge and the slopes are all finished and as soon as it snows I'm going to open up ———."

moss – something which belongs to your mother.

mote – a wide trench, filled with water, surrounding a castle.

motor – as in, "Is that going to be a ——— just a drainage ditch?"

mottle – a miniature construction of an original.

mountain – as in, "We will soon be ——— up to ride after them varmints."

mountain ash – as in, "I don't think that this is as big a ——— the last one we climbed."

mountain chain – a succession of metal rings, linked together, and used by climbers to swing from one precipice to another.

mountain dew – as in, "There ain't nothin' makes you feel so grand as a ———."

mountaineer – a loss of hearing caused by listening to too many yodellers.

mountain lion – as in, "Wow, that was some earthquake! Look, there's a ——— on its side over there."

mountaintop – a toy used by poor children living in the higher elevations.

mountebank – as in, "You can mount a horse, and you can mount a stair, but you can't ———."

mourner – as in, "I know not whether 'twas the beautiful ——— whether 'twas the gown she wore on that, our very first meeting."

mournful – as in, "You'll have to make an appointment for the afternoon. I already have the ———."

moustache – as in, "I——— this pot someplace where the fuzz won't look for it!"

mouthpiece – as in, "White man ———, but in heart he make ready for war!"

muddle

movable – as in, "Well, Sir, you're gonna have to get a pretty heavy trailer to ———."

movement – as in, "I wondered what that ——— when you jumped all six of my kings."

moving picture – as in, "It was Gloria, who, even while we were still ——— baby up and ran off into the woods with it."

mower – from the popular song, "——— than the greatest love the world has known."

Mr. – as in, "You can't throw spitballs at all. You ——— again."

mucus – as in, "The cat can't ——— I have my hand over its mouth."

muddle – as in, "This ——— ruin my brand new paint job." Also a football huddle on a wet day.

muddy – as in, "I'm sorry, Coach! When Kaslowski saw this ——— just screamed and ran for the dressing rooms."

muffle – as in, "Here, Dear, this ——— keep your hands warm!"

mule deer – as in, "I apologize for laughing, but when she sang she reminded me of our old ———."

multi – a method of preparing a hot drink.

mumble – a silent, male bovine animal.

muscat – as in, "I ——— a copy of today's paper."

mushroom – the place where you eat your morning cereal.

mushy – as in, "——— always act as though she's such a big deal?"

musketeer – a loss of hearing, prevalent among soldiers of the Continental Army who had been on the firing line too long.

muslin – as in, "Honey, what's the dog doing with his ——— my soup?"

mussel – as in, "I can tell you kids one thing, this ——— be picked up by dinnertime."

mustang – as in, "Here, hang up my horse. It's a ———, and a———, ——— somewhere!"

mustard gas – a disturbance of the intestines caused by eating too much of this condiment.

muster – as in, "When little Eva fell out of the apple tree she ——— new dress all up. And, incidentally, broke her leg."

mutilate – as in, "All right, you there, the third chair trumpet, you're using your ———."

mutineer – something which could happen to you if you stand in front of the trombone player and make uncomplimentary remarks.

mutinous – as in, "We, of the trumpet section, have decided that we don't like the bandmaster, Mister Purdley, anymore. He keeps ———."

mutiny – the action of resting a mute upon the middle leg joint, performed by musicians.

mutter – one who raises nondescript dogs.

mutton – as in, "Don't you put that ——— my new couch."

mystic – the proper way to address a young female, blood-sucking insect.

n

naive – as in, "'Tis well ———, and yet your work is not finished."

naphtha – as in, "The baby shouldn't be tired. What about the ——— she took this afternoon?"

narrate – as in, "Mi Lord says he ——— better fare, even in yon castle there."

naturalize – as in, "Many cosmeticians think that ———— look better than heavily shadowed ones."

nature – as in, "Hey ———— fly is open."

naughty – as in, "If he doesn't come to ———— will at best do very little in life."

naval – as the queen told Prince Valiant, "————, not tonight. Forsooth, I have a beastly headache."

Nazi – as in, "Grabbing them by the hair is ———— best way to get a girl."

nearly – as in, "I don't care if he's a scoundrel, Mother, I just want to be ————."

neat – as in, "I ———— someone to come in and clean."

neckband – Spooning with a group of musicians.

necktie – as in, "As we sat there and ———— began to wonder what I had got myself into."

nectar – as in, "I ———— up one side and down the other, and then while I was in the john she went home."

need – as in, "Hoping to defend herself she ———— him viciously."

needle – as in, "Those supplies we ———— be here Thursday."

negligee – one who neglects.

negligent – a man who neglects.

neighbor – a rare Ethiopian, male pig, which emits sounds like a donkey.

nematode – as in, "I finally figured out what to get my sisters for Christmas. I'm gettin' ————."

nemesis – as in, "Dear, since the boys don't have any other children to play with, maybe we should think about gettin' ————."

neon – as in, "If you put your ———— my back again I'll scream."

neophyte – as in, "Gal, get offa muh ———— is about to start."

Neptune – as in, "Hey, that's enough slow songs. Can't you guys play a————?"

nervous – as in, "You guys have got some ———— girls have been waiting here for three hours now."

nestle – as in, "Don't shake the tree. That hornets' ———— fall on your head!"

Nestor – as in, "Did this bird fall out of that ———— not?"

nettle – as in, "If you're really interested in catching butterflies, this ———— help."

network – as in, "I'm sorry, Captain, we'll have to return to port. We can't make the ————."

neuter – as in, "Hey, was that ———— Clyde that you were out with last night?"

neutral – as in, "If I'm gonna dig up any more of these tulip bulbs I'm gonna need a ————."

newborn – as in, "Hey, how do the cows like your ————?"

newly – as in, "That joke isn't very ————."

newness – as in, "Big Al says that if we get rid of Elliot they'll just get a ———— to replace him."

Newtonian – as in, "I'm just going to get a ———— then my hair will look better."

nicety – as in, "Hey, this is really a————." (Italian)

nickel – as in, "If you mugs try to leave the mob ———— rub you out."

nickname – as in, "Why on earth would ———— his kid Roquefort?"

nicotine – to gouge an adolescent.

niece – as in the popular song, "Climb upon my————, Sonny Boy."

night – a member of the Round Table.

nighthawk – clearing your throat after dark.

nightingale – as in, "I never thought I'd spend a ——— winds like this." Or, "King Authur, I caught this ———, your daughter's bedroom."

nightly – as in, "Giving that peasant the raspberry was not a ——— thing to do, Sir Mugwump."

nightmare – as in, "When the stallion gets horny he always has a ——— before retiring."

nightshade – dark glasses worn in the evening.

nighttime – the middle period of history called the dark ages.

nitric – what a hooker does after dark.

nitro – as in, "It's getting ——— faster or we'll never get back to the dock!"

nitrogen – an alcoholic drink made from juniper berries and nitric acid. It not only has an explosive quality in the stomach, but when a handkerchief is soaked in it and then allowed to dry, it's wonderful for blowing your nose. (off)

nobility – as in, "Why did you invite that deadbeat tenant over here this afternoon. This is ——— is going to settle."

noble – as in, "I think she's pregnant, and that's ———."

nocturne – a wooden container, with revolving paddles inside, and used for making butter. It makes a banging or thumping noise when in use.

node – as in, "If I had of ——— she was already pregnant I wouldn't have married her!"

noel – as in, "There may be a heaven but there ain't———."

nomad – as in, "I want your mother out of this house by sunset. I don't wanta spend the night with ——— woman"

no man's land – a woman pilot touching the runway.

noncom – not a communist.

nondescript – as in, "I fear, a——— must go. De story line is not too good."

none – a woman who lives in a convent.

noodle – as in, "If people think our art shows are dull this——— change their minds."

noose – as in, "No ——— is good ———."

Nordic – as in, "No, my girl, you are not going to elope with Tom, nor with Harry, ———."

normal – as in, "When you're ready to go ——— drive you to the station."

Norman – as in, "——— Sue are friendly, for being such weird people."

Norse – a naked horse.

nose – as in, "She——— that I love her, so why won't she marry me?"

notability – as in, "We don't put up with laziness, here at Goober Brothers, Inc., but we do ———."

notice – as in, "I think that this ——— from that girl who kept pinching me during choir practice."

notorious – as in, "This is Whig country. We don't want——— here."

novella – as in, "——— is going to run off with my little girl."

novelty – as in, "At four o'clock we were served a sumptuous repast of dried pelican eggs and barley cakes with yak butter, certainly a ———."

noxious – one who bangs on doors.

nuance – as in, "If you destroy all those ant hills we'll have to get some ———."

"Where is that patient the nursemaid run up and down the hall two hours after surgery?"

nuclear – as in, "We managed to get the giraffe and the elephant out of the zoo before the flood hit, but we couldn't get the ———."

nuisance – as in, "This rug must be ——— I was here last."

number – a very strong drink.

numerical – as in, "You're trying to tell me that you got pregnant without ever being with a man? Well, well. Looks like we got us a ———."

nunnery – as in, "So he wants to inherit my money, eh? Well, he may get ——— may get it all."

nursemaid – as in, "Where is that patient that the head ——— run up and down the hall two hours after surgery?"

nursery – as in, "The patient in 302 says that he'd better get that young, blonde ——— is going to refuse to vote for anymore hospital bonds."

nutcracker – a small wafer made from filberts.

nuthatch – as in, "The cat thinks that the walnut is an egg, and she's waiting to see the ———."

nutmeg – as in, "Oh, you're such a ———."

nutty – as in, "If he divorces that ——— will probably be a different fellow."

O

oaf – sound you make when someone punches you in the stomach.

oarlock – something the Harvard rowing team eats with cream cheese and bagels.

oasis – as in, "——— would be nice, but I'd rather have a little brother!"

obese – as in, "———— would be nice, I guess. Then we could have lots of honey."

occur – as in, "That's not a pedigreed dog, Martha. He's only ————."

ocelot – as in, "Isn't that the crazy saleswoman who sold ———— in the middle of a swamp?"

ocher – as in, "Is that tree an ———— is it a chestnut?"

octette – a cow with eight teats.

octopus – an eight-sided cat.

Oddfellow – a guy who's been to Sweden for an operation.

ode – as in, "Good Lord, I didn't think that we ———— that much!"

odor – as in, "So, I figured we could pay him what we ———— we could just skip town."

Odyssey – as Ulysses said while peering over the rail, "This is really an ————."

o'er – what you row a boat with.

offend – a position in football.

offense – as in, "We're going to have to put up ———— to keep those kids out of our pumpkin patch."

offer – as in, "My old aunt, Marian, married a man thirty years her junior and then, unfortunately, died on her wedding night. But it took them three days to get the smile ———— face!"

offhand – a crazy hired man.

officious – as in, "———— don't care. They just spawn right there in plain sight."

offset – a brand of TV which doesn't sell very well.

offspring – as in, "I did very well throughout the winter, but this has really been an ————."

octopus

ohm – where you live.

oil painting – a method of keeping works of art from squeaking.

oilskin – what you do to enable yourself to slip through a tight place.

oilslick – as in, "You'd better take your hands off that ———."

ointment – a salve for pigs throats.

O.K. – as in, "I see that you cut down the old ———."

okra – a little oak.

old English – elderly Londoners.

Old Glory – as in, "You tell ——— I ain't gonna be a hooker no more!"

old Nick – a Las Vegas odds-maker.

oldster – someone who collects these antique cars.

oleander – as in, "Yes ——— ran off last fall, which is why I think I'll divorce him."

olive – as in, "Yessum, ——— by mah own creed, which is to do it unto others 'fore they do it unto you!"

Olympus – as in, "The Raiders sack the quarterback as often as they can. ——— he back to the huddle a most embittered man." (anonymous)

omelet – as in, "After losing 96 to 3 ——— down, that's for sure!"

omen – as in, "——— are all right, I guess, but I would rather be an old maid than get married!"

once – as in, "I have plenty of fives but I need some more ———."

one – as in, "The game is over and we've ———."

one horse – as in, "The madam already left town, Sheriff, but ——— sitting in the middle of the street and she says she won't go!"

only – as in, "Hey, listen. He's your boyfriend, but you don't ———."

onslaught – placing a slot racer on the track.

onset – to be ready for filming.

onto – as in, "Okay, now remember, I'm gonna hike the ball ———."

onward – as in, "Why are you kids all jumping ———?"

ooze – as in, "A chorus of ——— went up from the crowd."

opal – as in, "If we can just score a touchdown perhaps ——— return to our fans!"

open – as in, "——— that's resting in my hand, and writing things I had not planned." (anonymous)

open-eyed – as in, "If her door were ——— go in and propose to her!"

opera – as in, "She's gonna ——— freight tonight, and get outta here."

operate – as in, "Maw, some guy at the ——— my popcorn while I was watching this yere Aida."

operator – as in, "Well, Doc, are you gonna ——— just stand there?"

opiate – as in, "I haven't seen their pet goat around this year. I think that ——— her."

opossum – as in, "——— me the bottle and we'll have another round."

oppose – as in, "His hard exterior was just ———"

oppressor – as in, "——— body close and she'll be putty in your hands."

opulent – as in, "I ———— Fred that twenty that he needed."

orate – what you pay per hour for oars.

ordeal – as in, "She ain't much of a prostitute, that's fer shore. But in a game of poker, just watch that ————."

ordinance – as in, "The only place I ever see any of those little insects is over here at your place. Tell me, are you ————?"

ordinary – as in, "Nope, I ain't ———— thing except what the government says I can have."

organ – a Western State.

organism – extreme sexual excitement.

organize – as in, "The man sitting by the ———— the preacher strangely from time to time."

orgy – as in, "You yell 'haw' when you want the mule to turn to the left, ———— to the right."

origin – as in, "I guess that I'll have a stinger, ———— and tonic."

original sin – as in, "I think that we'd better lock these ———— the vault over night."

ornate – as in, "She doesn't care whether she sleeps with Jack, ———— or Fred, or Harry, or Burt, or Gideon, or the men's glee club, or the Ram's backfield, or the Army Reserve, or . . . ."

oscillate – as in, "For God's sake, Fred, hurry up. You're going to make ———— for the party."

ostracize – as big as an ostrich.

otter – as in, "We ———— be gettin' along home now."

ought – as in, "It's certainly ———— in'ere." (Cockney)

ouija – as in, "———— like a cookie, little girl?"

outcropping – as in, "We wouldn't give the goat any pancakes and so now he's ——— grass in back of the barn."

outdated – as in, "Since she became the only woman in the fire department she has ——— every woman I've ever known."

outgoing – as in, "The Judge's kidneys ain't too good, so there'll be a short recess while he's ———."

outlander – as in, "She may be good at getting a plane off the ground, but I can ———."

outlaw – as in, "What would society be with ———?"

outstanding – as in, "She was in there, in front of a roaring fire with Dick, while I was ——— in the cold."

outward – as in, "I've heard all of that sort of talk I want to. You'd better get ——— before I lose my temper."

outweigh – as in, "I want to go ——— out where the buffalo roam, and the deer and the antelope play."

oval – as the queen said to Prince Valiant, when he surprised her with her lover, "———, I didn't expect you 'til tomorrow."

overbearing – as in, "If you have 23 children, Mrs. Glick, I'd say that you are ———."

overhanging – as in, "The sheriff will be back in a minute, Ma'am. He's ——— your old man right now."

overrate – as in, "I don't feel too good. I think that I ———."

overture – as in, "Hey, let's go ——— house and show this mouse to your sister."

ox – sounds emitted by crows.

Oxford – as in, "Can your ——— the stream with the water this high?"

oxidate – as in, "Yes, the genie gave 'im a solid gold date palm. Now when 'e's a little bit short why 'e just ———!"

oxidize – as in, "Paw, I shore hope we get this wagon to Californy before the ———."

oxygen – as in, "If you want to see something really funny, give your ——— and tonic."

oyster – as in, "I know that she's fat, but let's try to ——— up on the truck."

P

pace – as in, "It ——— to keep your eyes open around here!"

pact – as in, "Are you ——— yet?"

paddle – as in, "This ——— do for the time being, but I wouldn't want to live here all year!"

paddy – as in, "After he saw my ——— went outside and threw up."

padlock – for securing your pad.

padre – as in, "Where did you find this seed ———?"

paean – as in, "After a twelve-hour bus ride the team spent a few blessed minutes out in back ———."

page – as in, "I ——— yer paw fer ya, and yer my missus now!"

pagoda – as in, "Maw, why did ——— town without us?"

painful – an intricately constructed window.

painstaking – removing glass from windows.

pair – an edible fruit.

palace – as in, "My ———— goin' to be here in a minute, and then you'd better watch out!"

palate – as in, "My ———— everything in the refrigerator and then started going through the kitchen cabinets."

palaver – what a traffic cop says when he wants you to come to a stop.

pale – a utensil for carrying water.

pale face – a man with a bucket over his head.

palette – as in, "My ———— a bucket of raw oysters in only seven minutes."

palfrey – as in, "If the warden don't set my ———— I'm gonna set off this here dynamite, and blow up the guard's john!"

paling – collecting water in pails.

palisade – as in, "My ———— there's more gold in them hills than you can shake a stick at."

pall – a man's name.

pall bearer – as in, "She's such an idiot. How can ————?"

pallor – as in, "Well, my dear, are you looking for a ———— a lover?"

palsy – as in, "Did ———— what you did to his new car?"

Panama – as in, "Hand me that ————."

panda – as in, "You're wrong, my friend. In all my years as a critic on this paper I have never ———— really good play!"

pander – as in, "I ———— book because it was trash, not because she rejected me."

pandora – as in, "How about a nice game of ————?"

panel – as in, "This ———— never do, it's much too small!"

panetela – as in, "It is the bank's policy never to hire people over eight feet tall. Therefore, we can never make Mr. ———."

pang – a loud report.

panicky – as in, "All your finger paints have really made this ———."

pannikin – a store dummy made from dish pans.

pansy – as in, "You've really got an ugly ———."

pantheon – as in, "Here, Sweetheart, you'd better put your ———."

panther – as in, "Thith ith motht embarrathing, thir. Pleath, hand me my ——— and I'll be on my way."

pantry – a store that sells pants.

paper – as in, "If you're going to work for me there's one thing you should understand. Around here we ——— item sold."

paperhanger – one of those stupid excuses for garment hangers which have recently replaced the old metal ones.

paper weight – as in, "As far as I'm concerned, the editor is a dummy, and you can just let the ——— for it's story."

paper work – as in, "If plywood isn't strong enough, then why would ———?"

paprika – as in, "I can always tell when our father's been out drinking because ——— of whiskey."

parable – as in, "Don't you know anything about hitching up a team? you can't ——— with a jackass."

parachute – as in, "If you should see that ——— 'em down like dogs."

paradise – used in shooting craps.

paradox – as in, "If you don't want to buy any warehouses, how about a ———." Also pertaining to two doctors.

paragon – as in, "Now where on earth have that ————?"

paragraphs – two long-necked animals.

parallel bars – two saloons, side by side.

paralyze – as in, "You told me a ————, Bertha, and I'm going to get even with you, if it's the last thing I do!"

paramount – as in, "You'd better pre———— for Sir Charles."

paramour – as in, "You may a———— charming to them, but I can see right through you!"

paranoia – as in, "Excuse me, Madam, but does this ————?"

parapets – two dogs, two cats, two alligators, etc.

paraphernalia – as in, "Mother wants the manicure scissors so that she can ————."

parasite – as in, "We'd better pre———— for the tiger wrestling contest!"

parasynthesis – as the Devil once remarked about liquor and sex, "What a ————."

parcel – as in, "If you can't shoot under ———— your clubs and take up bowling."

parch – a cross between a pine and a larch. Also an exterior addition to a building.

pardon – as in, "I don't know why you ever took up golf. That last hole you shot 15 over ————."

pare – as in, "Yes, they certainly make a ————."

parfait – as in, "You just shut up about my golf game. Maybe I want to shoot over ————."

Pariah – as in, "That's the ———— told you about earlier."

Paris – as in, "My ———— higher than your pair, so I win!"

parka – as in, "You idiot. That's no way to ———— car."

parquet – as in, "Okay, it's settled. We'll meet you in the ————."

parrot – as in, "Here, take this apple and ———."

parry – how you look after having pears thrown at you.

parted – as in, "You picked up the wrong ———."

partial – as in, "If she ever shoots under ——— have a stroke."

party – something used to hold your golf ball, when you shot par on the last hole.

party line – what a guy says to girls at parties.

pasha – as in, "You'll never ——— test without cheating."

passable – as in, "No, this mule can't get past a horse, but he can ———."

passage – a woman's age when men make passes at her.

passe – as in, "It looks like snow so we'd better hurry and get over the ———."

passenger – as in, "Are you kidding? You've been ——— favors out to every guy in town!"

passion – as in, "Thish ish the only way to get through the ———."

passionate – as in, "This is the story of an unfortunate young man who, blinded by ——— a home-cooked meal, prepared by his girlfriend, and died shortly thereafter."

passion fruit – as in, "Hey, ——— down to me, will ya."

passion play – as in, "Here's to those, wrinkled, old and gray, who still at games of ———." (anonymous)

passive – a quarterback with a team that can't run up the middle.

Passover – as in, "You'd better ——— that bottle, you hear?"

passport – to offer around a glass of wine.

paste – as in, "It ——— to be ignorant."

pastel – as in, "No, you took the wrong turn after you left the Pearly Gates, and about two miles back you ———."

pastor – as in, "She ——— husband on the freeway."

pastoral – as in, "If you do that in church the ——— throw you out on your ear!"

pastry – something which strippers wear on their breasts.

pasture – as in, "Hey, Al, I just ——— wife coming out of a dirty book store."

pate – as in, "Yes, early this morning she ——— her bill and checked out."

pater – as in, "I ——— twenty in advance, and while I was in the john she left."

path – as in, "No, I think that I'll ——— for now."

pathway – as in, "I think that driver is drunk! You'd better ——— over to the left!"

patio – as in, "And this is my good friend, ———Malley."

patter – as in, "As he reached over to ——— hand she suddenly bit him."

pattern – as in, "How much money does ——— now?"

paunch – as in, "He's not a scientific boxer, but he delivers quite a ———."

pause – as in, "I think that ——— out in back of the hen house with a jug!"

pawn – as in, "Up——— hearing this, she let out a wail and collapsed."

pawnee – one who frequents hock shops.

peace – a vegetable, having small, round, green edible seeds.

peaceful – to be full of peas.

peacemaker – as in, "Don't you have some other vegetable? ——— sick."

peace pipe – a long tube used in canneries down which peas roll.

pea fowl – as in, "I will not eat this vegetable. Carrots are all right, but I find a ———."

pea jacket – a pod.

peal – as in, "I'll bet that this last ——— be too much for you to eat!"

peanut – as in, "I'm going into the men's room because I've gotta ———."

peasant – as in, "My, what a ——— little place you have here!"

peat – a man's name.

pecan – as in, "Eating a ——— make you sick!"

peccadillo – a mechanical sexual aid for chickens.

peccary – active, used in reference to chickens.

pectin – as in "Those stupid chickens have ——— the front door."

pectoral – as in, "She lay in the barnyard, a pitiful sight, while dozens of chickens ——— night." (anonymous)

pedagogue – as the baby said when it saw the puppy, "Me wanta ———."

pedal – as in, "No matter how much time you have, you can't ——— those animals!"

pedicure – as in, "That new vet stopped my dog from hiccoughing. Maybe he can give your ———."

Pegasus – as in, "——— not to worry. We didn't much care for that lamp anyhow."

pegleg – that upon which Peggy stands.

peignoir – as in, "I wrote for so long a time that after a while my ——— out."

Pekingese – as in, "If we can't watch the girls through the front windows maybe we can ———."

"She lay in the barnyard, a pitiful sight,
while dozens of chickens pectoral night."

pelvis – used to be a rock singer.

penal – of the male organ.

pencil – as in, "If they keep bringin' in cattle the holding —— be full by midnight."

pendulous – as in, "Hey, June, is this the ——?"

penetrate – as in, "When he writes with a —— shows up that is not apparent in his typing."

penny – a small pen.

Pentecost – as in, "How much did your Ford ——?"

peon – as in, "Who put this —— my plate?"

people – a stake which a pea vine grows up.

pepper pot – an unpleasantly spicy form of marijuana.

pepsin – doing something wrong with a cheerleader.

peradventure – as in, "Don Juan received a different social disease ——."

percent – as in, "These perfumes are ten dollars ——."

perchance – as in, "Step right up. Only twenty five cents ——."

percussion – as in, "Naw, I've heard a lot of swearing in my time, and that was some pretty ——."

perdition – as in, "Take Grandma back to the kitchen and keep —— out that stew."

peregrine – as in, "In all my born days I've never seen such a ——horns before."

perforates – as in, "Let's go to another motel. We're too —— like these."

perhaps – as in, "We all got out of the house safely except for —— mother who was stuck in the john."

periphrases – as in, "That's a —— I don't ever want to hear you say again."

perish – an ecclesiastical district.

periwinkle – as in, "I thought that she liked me when I saw ——— at me."

permeate – as in, "Everyone else went out for hamburgers while ——— lobster and champagne at home."

permit – something an outfielder doesn't want.

peroxide – as in, "I've been buying hides for years, and I'm telling you, that's a ———." Also, "In this flat country, where could a ———?"

perpetual – as in, "I've never seen a dog that bites so much. Yessir, that certainly is a ——— have."

perpetuate – as in, "I'll have you know, Sir, that was no wild fowl. That was the child's ———."

Persian – as in, "You can't say 'man' kind anymore. You have to say ———."

person – as in, "Yes, he escaped unharmed, but his ——— and daughter were carried off, howling, by Bigfoot."

personage – as in, "It is an incident like this that will make a ——."

personal – as in, "I hate to tell you this, but you are really a lousy ———."

personate – as in, "Some ——— my blueberry pie, and I think it was you."

personnel – as in, " ——— , it was the dog that ate your blueberry pie!"

perspire – as in, "You call yourself an architect? Look at the steeple you designed for this church. Frankly, I've never seen such a ———."

persuade – as in, "I wouldn't wear these shoes to a dog fight. That is very ———!"

peruse – as in, "Wearing that ape suit got you into the zoo free, but from the looks of those zoo attendants, it may turn out to be a very ———."

perverse – as in, "He's not much of a poet. This is very ———."

pesky – what the landlord uses to to unlock your apartment.

peso – as in, "If you understood prices down here you wouldn't ——— much."

pestilent – "That ——— me his old lawnmower while he's using my brand new gasoline one."

pet cock – act performed by those fond of roosters.

petrify – to inundate someone with cats and dogs.

petrol – a sleeping bag for dogs.

petticoat – as in, "Oh yes, animal velly fliendly with children. Perhaps they likee ———."

pettish – fond of small, domesticated animals.

petty – a girl's name.

phaeton – as in, "I guess that marrying him is just your ——— there's nothing you can do about it."

phallus – as in, "Hey, ———, wait for me."

phantasm – a phantom orgasm.

Pharaoh – a litter of pigs.

Pharisee – as in, "Did anyone at the ——— you lose your pants?"

pharmacy – as in, "I don't want to live in the city anymore. I'm going to buy a place in the country and be a ———."

phase – as in, "Is this the ——— that launched a thousand ships?"

pheasant – a rustic, or a counry person of inferior social rank.

philander – as in, " ——— said they were going to stay overnight, and now they've been here for a week."

191

Philippine – as in, "Jack and —— over behind that bush."

philosopher – as in, "I think that —— no reason at all. He was way ahead of everyone else, and then he just quit."

phlox – as in, "There were —— of sheep on every hill."

Phoebe – as in, "How much will your —— ?"

phosphorus – as in, "None of the other teachers like the idea of us kids putting a bar in the student union, but Mr. ——."

photoengrave – to take a picture of someone's last rites.

photoplay – as in, "I expect to see this —— a prime role in trapping the suspect!"

phrase – as in, "Everytime it rubs against the stone, the rope —— a little more."

Phyllis – as in, "For many hours thereafter they proceeded to —— with wine and sweetmeats."

physique – a purge or cathartic.

piastre – as in, "Old Hap—— to go to bed with him, and that was when she hit him."

piazza – as in, "This —— very strange flavor."

pica – as in, "You're only a ——. I ate twice as much as you did."

picador – as in, "I don't know what room she's in. Just —— and knock."

picayune – as in, "Y'all —— self a spot and set awhile, hear?"

piccalilli – as in, "What are you doing here? You're supposed to —— up at five o'clock."

piccolo – as in, "You can pick high, and you can ——,but you can't pick no finer cotton than this."

pickle – as in, "This —— never work! It's too light!"

"He wasn't very good at washing clothes, but you should have seen that pig iron."

picnic – as in, "I want you to drive over to the school and —— up."

picture – as in, "I —— wife up in Joe's Bar, so whatta ya think of them apples?"

piebald – a hairless pastry.

piece – that which comes between wars.

pierce – as in, "To be tried by a jury of one's ——."

pigeonhole – as in, "Don't use a 12 gauge shotgun on that bird. I want that ——."

pig iron – as in, "Yes, I trained him from the time he was just a piglet. He wasn't very good at washing clothes, but you should have seen that ——."

pigment – as in, "Until you've butchered them all, you'll never know just how much a ——."

pigtail – a story about a pig.

pilaster – what your walls are covered with.

pile – as in, " —— means, come right in."

pile driver – as in, "Watch out for that wood——."

pilfer – as in, "I feel really weird. What did I take that —— ?"

pillory – as in, "Either he took that —— fell asleep without it."

pilot – as in, "Just bring that stuff in and —— right here."

pimpernel – as in, "She didn't know he was a —— would never have gone with him."

pinafore – as in, "I don't know what number she's supposed to be. Just —— on her and hope that it's right."

pincers – as in, "This —— is the very one which, dipped in poison, was used to murder old Nutley."

pinion – as in, "What is Europe—— of our foreign policy?"

pinnace – as in, "This ——— too small to hold up my bloomers."

pinochle – caused by getting your hand in the way when you're passing water.

pint – as in, "Just tell me. It's rude to ———." (Texan).

pinto – a wrestling hold.

pioneer – what you probably have after a pie-throwing contest.

pious – as in, "Um, boy. Those ——— sure do smell good."

pipe dream – what you have after being mugged with a pipe.

pique – as in, "We weren't doin' nothin'. We just wanted to ——— into the girls' restroom."

pirate – the price you pay for pies.

pistol – as in, "I drank so much beer that I bet I can ——— daylight."

pistoleer – a condition caused by firing one's weapon too close to the head.

pistol grip – a suitcase full of pistols.

piston – as in, "Hey, Mack, somebody just ——— the front porch."

pitchy – irritable and abrupt.

piteous – as in, "The ——— that it needn't have happened at all."

pithy – as in, "What a ——— your mother couldn't have been here to see this."

pittance – as in, "If you're really getting bored, we might play war and ——— against beetles."

pity – as in, "Then, after he fell into the ——— couldn't get out."

pixy – as in, "Using one of the ——— managed to break a hole through the wall."

pizzicato – as in, "These olive —— be the hardest things to get out that I've ever seen."

place – as in, "Yes, and when he sits down at the piano he —— so well."

place kick – as in, "As soon as he gets into —— his chair out from under him."

placer – as in, "No, I don't want you in the orchestra! You simply can't ——."

plain – an aircraft.

planter – as in, "She died Thursday, and tomorrow we're gonna ——."

playful – as in, "Is the ——, or can I still get a seat?"

playground – as in, "In the second act the —— slowly to a halt."

plier – as in, "Once in my apartment, I proceeded to —— with booze."

plutocrat – one who admires Mickey Mouse's dog.

pneumonia – as in, "You must have been to the bank. That looks like —— got there."

poach – a slang expression for a dog.

pod – as in, "Oh, I couldn't let you do that, Ferdy. —— skin me alive if'n he found out."

podium – as in, "You will also receive additional monies on a —— basis."

pogrom – as in, "How do you like our musical —— so far?"

poinciana – as in, "I'm punishing you because it's bad manners to ——."

poise – as in, "——, ——, if you must fight, go outside."

poison – as in, "No, we didn't get all the kids yet, Miss Mudlark. There are two —— top of the schoolhouse."

poker – as in, "Maybe she's dead! ——— and see."

pokeweed – as in, "If we had any gold in our ——— get out of here."

polar bear – as in, "In last year's parade when we pulled her float she was wearing only a bikini and this year she wants us to ———."

polarize – as in, "Mommy, Jane grabbed my doll and tried to ——— out."

polecat – as in, "How am I gonna get you down off of that ———?"

police – as in, "You should have consulted a lawyer before you signed any agreement. This is a very ——— you have here!"

policy – as in, "Did ——— who stole her pet pig?"

polish – as in, "Bartender, I shink my friend ——— drunk."

polite – as in, "Don't you have any bigger bulbs? That's a very ———."

pollen – as in, "I just saw ——— Terry coming out of the girl's dorm."

poll tax – used to attach posters to telephone poles.

polonaise – a dance performed on horseback.

pomade – as in, "That ——— a nice looking addition to the yard."

pomander – as in, "My sister put some of that stuff on her ——— skin turned all red."

pomegranate – as in, "Only the statue in the park has a ———."

pompadour – as in, "Hey, Boss, if he won't come out of there why don't we ——— full of lead!"

pompous – as in, "I don't think these girls really like us. I think they're spies and they're trying to ———."

pontiff – as in, "There won't be any water in the ——— this drought keeps up."

pony – as in, "The only thing wrong with your figure gal is you ain't got no legs. Now looka here. That's a ——— if I ever saw one!"

pool – as in, "Beat it kid or Winnie the ——— hibernate on you."

popcorn – the guy who taught me how to write gags like these.

popinjay – an expression of disgust, as in, "Get this bubblegum ——— out of here." (Used only among birds.)

poplar – as in, "She was very ——— at school."

popover – as in, "Why don't we have ——— for dinner."

popper – as in, "If she gives you any back talk, ———."

poppet – as in, "See that guy's balloon? Let's get a pin and ———."

poppied – as in, "I told ——— better quit drinking 'cause the preacher's coming."

poppy – as in, "Mother said to tell ——— has to take us to town."

poppycock – a rooster who's head of a family.

populace – as in, "Hey, ——— out some good sounds for such a square cat."

populate – as in, "Hey, ———. All the gang left hours ago."

porcine – as in, "I don't mind some billboards, but that is really a ———."

porcupine – an expression used among lumberjacks, meaning to grease a pine tree with pork fat.

pore – as in, " ——— me a strong one, bartender."

pornographic – an expression used by the town council upon discovering that the street department laid concrete sidewalks with dirty illustrations them. "We don't ——— sidewalks in this town."

porpoise – as in, "And what is your ——— here, Sir?"

port – as in, "I ——— out all your whiskey, Grandpa, 'cause Mommy needed a bottle."

portal – as in, "This bottle of ——— knock you on your ear."

portent – as in, "Why did you buy such a ———, Harvey? Now it's raining and coming in all the holes."

portfolio – something carried by a wine salesman.

porthole – as in, "I hope you didn't break that wine bottle. I like my ———."

portion – from an old radio serial, " ——— faces life."

Portland – as in, "Never mind how badly the car is wrecked, where did that bottle of ——— ?"

portly – as in, "I think it was ——— my fault."

portrait – as in, "Stupidity is a very——— in a politician."

portray – as in, "I think that you're going to win this hand. All I've got is one ———."

Portuguese – a nautical instruction for directing the flock to the left.

posse – as in, "Come here ——— cat."

possum – as in, "Jewels are my downfall, Dahling. I simply cahn't ——— up, you know."

post – as in, "Yes, his presence here has ——— quite a problem for us."

postage – length of time it takes a letter to reach its destination. (if it ever does)

postal – as in, "Yes, that——— be big enough. Let's pull it up."

postdate – mail-order dating.

post haste – something lacking in the U.S. Post Office.

postmaster – as in, "Why not tie your horse to this ——— ."

postpone – a bread made of cornmeal and delivered by mail.

postulate – as in, "You would have been the winner if I hadn't ———— in the race."

posture – as in, "I didn't know you were home until I ———— house."

post war – as in, "The ———— out and we had to get another one."

potato bug – a listening device placed in vegetables.

potency – as in, "I wouldn't drink any more of that if I were you, Sir. It's very ————."

pot hole – a place to stash your marijuana.

pot pie – a dish by A. Toklas.

prairie – a place where very devout people go to commune with their creator.

prairie dog – someone you got on a blind date in Wyoming.

praise – as in, "I don't know if he's a religious man, but he ———— a lot."

prank – a large, sturdy board. (Japanese)

prate – as in, "————tell, good Sir, what light shines from yon window?"

prattle – as in, "If you keep falling down on the ice your ———— get sore."

precede – turning over the soil in preparation for planting.

precedent – the head of our country.

precious – as in, "And with these words of love she ———— him to her bosom and they both fall out of bed."

precise – sounds your lover makes before embracing.

predate – a rendezvous with someone in the afternoon when you have another date later that night.

prefer – as in, "Yes, we press these boards out of fir now, but this one here is ———."

preparatory – as in, "We can't let a Whig become President. We've got to ———."

presence – as in, "I hope that I get some ——— this Christmas."

pressure – as in, "You'd better ——— pants before you go out."

pretend – as in, "Yes, I ——— here before the regular bartender comes on."

prey – as in, " ——— tell me, what are you doing here?"

price – as in, "I ——— myself on being a good judge of character."

pride – as in, "Why have you continually ——— into my affairs?"

primary – as in, "This is my affair and you shouldn't ———."

primate – as in, "Actually, I'm living with three different girls. There's Suzie, and Wendy, but Donna is my ———."

primer – as in, "This pump's pretty old. We may have to ———."

primeval – as the queen said to Prince Valiant on their wedding night, "Don't be so hasty! First I need a drink to ———."

prince – as in, "Inspector, I think that we have him now. His ——— are all over this room!"

princess – as in, "The ——— he's stuck in his armor and needs some assistance."

prior – as in, "Is that girl gonna come out here or do I have to go in and ——— loose myself."

prism – a building which houses convicts.

privateer – as in, "And upon hearing these words she shed a———."

prize – as in, "I'll never be happy here. Aunt Ellen continually ——— into my affairs."

procedure – as in, "Don't worry none about that football scout son. If that ——— passin' ability he's gonna sign you up fer shore."

process – as in, "The tennis ——— that I'm improving."

procreate – as in, "Why did the ——— such a fuss? All I did was sling my driver through the clubhouse window."

procure – as in, "Naw, Coach. I'm not hurt. But I think that I — football that you gimme!"

prodigal – as in, "Yeah, you can get most birds to fly when you want 'em to, but you've to to ———."

proffer – as in, "What the heck did you have to go see a———? I could have shown you how to hit that little ball, Nellie."

profit – as in, "Well, ——— doesn't make much difference if you flunk me. I've got to leave school anyway since I got little Lulu in trouble."

profound – as in, "We can't go to the country club anymore since the ——— us making out in the locker room."

prologue – as in, "Did the ——— my hole in one on the bulletin board?"

promise – as in, "If you're going to the ——— , you'd better start getting ready."

pronouns – as in, "I'm strictly against adjectives and verbs, but I am ———."

propaganda – as in, "This country is spending fantastic sums of money to help the underdeveloped African nations, and now we've got to ——— up."

proper – as in, "Of course she's sober enough to marry me judge. Just ———— up and let's get on with the ceremony!"

property – as in, "Oh, not those old tinned biscuits, Mum. I want this to be a ————."

proportion – as in, "You're not playing college ball now, Boy. We want our players to eat plenty and keep their strength up! Now take that tray back and get yourself a ————."

prorate – what call girls charge you.

prose – professionals.

protectorate – as in, "If inflation keeps on, the town hooker is going to raise her prices. We've got to do something to ————."

protein – as in, "No, I like little kids, and I'm very ————."

protest – something which rookies go through in training camp.

protract – as in, "Yes, we've had a lot of well-known players buy into our development. Now here is another ————."

prowl – as in, "Mister Simms, if you don't ring the engine room and order all engines stopped, our ———— be stuck halfway into that dock."

Prussian – a proud Russian.

psalm – as in, "———— body stole my gal."

Psalter – as in, "Jenny's having trouble with her food, Dear. Would you ———— meat for her."

pshaw – a title for Iran's ruler.

psychic – as in, "Yes, he's been my partner and ———— for years."

ptarmigan – as in, "I don't mind being ridden out of town on a rail, but are you going to feather and ———— ?"

ptomaine – as in, "Paul Bunyan was so big that he could stand with New Hampshire under his heel and under his————."

public – what your dog does when you spill beer on the floor of an English tavern.

publican – as in, "That's right! I've been down at the ———— up as much beer as I can hold."

pucker – to strike a woman with a hockey puck.

pudding – as in, "I will be ———— the scores on the board as they arrive."

puff adder – as in, "I ran so hard to tell her the news that by the time I got to the house all I could do was ————."

puffball – overly energetic lovemaking which leaves you out of breath.

puffin – half of what the Big Bad Wolf did.

puffy – "After just one ———— ran to the window and shouted, 'I can fly, I can fly.' "

pullet – as in, "And then she took hold of my sweatshirt and began to ———— off."

pulley – as in, "After one ———— dropped the hookah and shouted, 'You fooled me young Lady! That's not tobacco! It's that abominable hemp.'"

Pullman – as in, "Hey, we're never gonna get the car out of the ditch unless you ————."

pulpit – as in, "Take this orange and ————."

pulse – as in, "Listen, my column ———— in a lot of advertising."

pumpkin – trying to get information out of relatives.

pun – as in, "A ———— this page I write in jest and there a ———— I do invest."

puncheon – as in, "Stop ———— me or I'll tell the teacher!"

punctual – as in, "Listen ———— better clear out of here before I lose my temper!"

pungent – a fellow who uses words so as to produce a different meaning with a humorous effect.

punish – fond of making up puns, frequently engaging in wordplay.

pupil – medicine you swallow in church.

puppet – a young dog.

puppy – as in, "When George saw the size of the ——— screamed and ran out the door."

purchase – as in, "Well, Old Boy, I've ridden to the hounds many times, but today was really a ———."

pure – as in, "A——— nose."

purely – "I don't think this girl is very ———."

purloin – as in, "I'm taking this meat back to the butcher. I've never seen such a ———."

purple – poor people.

purport – a bad place to take shore leave.

purpose – something a photographer has to put up with.

purse – sounds of satisfaction made by a cat.

pursue – as in, "———, she thought he was going to marry her until she caught him with Edna."

pursuit – something bought from a cut-rate clothier.

purview – as in, "Tell the desk clerk I wish to be moved at once. This room has a very ———."

pussyfoot – what you use to kick the cat.

puttee – as in, "After he made the——— seemed to go berserk and ran screaming down the hill."

putting green – not experienced in sinking a golfball.

pylon – as in, "Even though he no longer had the ball, everyone began to ———."

pyramid – as in, "After years of this self-indulgence, her mind began to go, and sometimes she would a———— her dinner guests wearing nothing but a smile."

pyre – as in, "All right, do you want more ———— not?"

pyrite – as in, "After all these years of baking, Marcia, you'd think that you could at least bake a mince ————."

Pythian – as in, "My thithter will be out in jutht a minute. She'th in the bathroom ————."

Python – a pie eating contest.

q

quack – as in, "I've been an animal psychiatrist for many years, but this is the first time I've ever seen a duck ———— up."

quadrangle – a task performed by four cowboys.

quadrant – to carry on and rave in jail.

quadrate – what it cost the taxpayers to maintain the jail.

quadrille – as the author was once told by a judge, "We're gonna put you in the ————."

quadroon – as in, "Why did that guy we had in the ———— the lace curtains the sheriff's wife put there?"

quadruple – a Russian coin worth four times the standard monetary unit.

quail – as in, "Why don't we take ———— the men's shore privileges," the Captain said.

quaker – as in, "After the ———— mother was still insisting that the end of the world had come!"

quart – as in, "When the king spoke, the ladies of the ———— all giggled."

"This is the first time I've ever seen a duck quack up."

quarter – as in, "I would like to ——— but I'm afraid of her father." Also one who divides liquids into fourths.

quarter back – as in, "I knew a lady who spent $30,000 to send her son to college, and all she got was a ———."

quarterly – as in, "No, we'd better buy a ——— will drink it all up before we have any."

quartz – as in, "The ——— have been very lenient with you up 'til now."

quasi – as in, "I don't think he was really a hunchback ——— looked different sometimes."

quaver – a member of the society of friends.

quay – as in the popular southern song, "Look ———, look ———, look ——— Dixie Land."

queen – as in, "That soap was terrific! Look, I'm ———, I'm ———!"

quench – as in, "Who is that black ——— in the third row?"

query – as in, "Your brother doesn't have any sense! Look——— left his roller skates."

quest – as in, The famous words of Horace Greeley, when he said, "Look ——— young man, look ———." (Note: Greeley stayed back East with the girls.)

questionable – seeking to obtain information from a male bovine animal.

question mark – as in, "That was the answer, now what was your ———?"

quibble – as in, "If you rock the baby so hard his ——— fall over."

quicken – a cross between a quail and a chicken.

quicksand – as in, "——— the fender. We have to get the car repaired and painted again before Father gets home."

quill – as in, "A little luck ——— not hurt us either."

quipped – as in, "I think we're better e——— to handle this problem."

quire – those who sing in a church.

quixotic – one who always sings in exotic keys.

quorum – as in, "Take these apples and ———."

rabbet – a wager with the rabbi.

rabbi – as in, "I don't know who that lady was! She ——— me so fast I couldn't tell!"

rabies – baby rays.

race – as in, "There she stood in the ——— of the setting sun."

racer – as Buck Rodgers said, "You'd better hand me that ———."

racial – as in, "If mother sees ——— throw a fit."

racket – as in, "I'm sorry abour your car, Mr. Bernstein! We were going to grease it, but while it was up on the ——— fell off!"

racy – as in, "Did ——— his picture in the paper?"

radial – as in, "They were his cards, so why didn't ——— first?"

radiant – as in, "Did you show ——— we found in da kitchen?"

raffia – as in, "Anymore talk like that, young lady, and I'm gonna ——— off to the highest bidder!"

ragamuffin – to tease a muffin unmercifully.

rage – as in, "Wait a minute, I think that ——— just got home."

raglan – a country where nothing but ragtime music is heard.

rag tag – a game in which the players tear to shreds the clothes of the one who is "it."

rail – as in, "He's a ——— Texan all right!"

railhead – someone who smokes a lot of pot.

rainy – as in, "After it began to ——— took off his clothes and began dancing around the backyard."

raise – something belonging to Ray.

raisin – as in, "If the Boss doesn't give me a ——— the morning I'm quitting!"

rake-off – as in, "Hey, get your ——— my foot."

rally – as in, "I love your new dress, Dahling, ——— I do!"

ram's horn – something which sounds in the locker room of the Los Angeles football team.

ramshackle – a device used to restrict the movements of male sheep.

rancho – as in, "Oh they're going to take your ——— they're going to take your ranch!"

random – as in, "Yeah, you got the ball fine, Koslewski, but after that you ———."

rangy – as in, "One morning, while out riding the ——— fell off his horse into a pool of it; and that's how the Colonel discovered oil!"

rank – a place to skate in Texas.

ransack – to have participated in a sack race.

ransom – as in, "First we walked for awhile, and then we ———.'

rap – the upper portion of your legs and lower abdomen. (Chinese)

rapid – as in, "Mother, Johnny was bad in school today and the teacher ——— his knuckles."

ratchet

rapport – as in, "Well, this is the place. Should we ——— ring the bell?"

rapt – as in, "He, unknown'st behind her'd stand, and with his ruler ——— her hand." (anonymous)

rapture – as in, "After he went berserk, I ——— husband up in his sleeping bag and tied it to a tree."

rare – as in, "How do you like this warm summer ——— ?"

rarity – as in, "It was a ——— during which my mother did not try to sing for her guests."

rasher – as in, "Is that a ——— does your face always look like that?"

raspberry – as in, "I hope you find my tools. I liked that ——— much."

ratchet – a cross between a rake and a hatchet.

rate – as in, "I'm sorry I'm so ———." (Japanese)

rattail – the story of the Pied Piper.

rattan – as in "Boy, it must have taken a lot of sun to make your white ——— like that."

rattle – as in, "If he gets away that little ——— ruin everything."

raven – as in, "He's been ——— like that for hours."

razor – as in, "It's either ——— Ed's, I think."

real – as in, "As she considered his words her mind began to ———."

realize – as in, "No, I don't wear contact lenses. These are my ———."

realtor – as in, "One day my mother-in-law fell off the boat. Everyone thought it was a whale and she nearly got harpooned. Finally, we got a cable over a winch and ——— in."

rear guard – the book a kid puts into his pants when he thinks he may get spanked.

rebate – as in, "That darned fish got my worm again. I'll have to ——— my hook."

recant – as in, "My mother says that Ma——— come out now."

recede – as in, "Now that the rains have stopped I guess we'll have to ——— this field."

recess – as in, "Ma——— she'll have to see you some other time."

recital – as in, "Yep, the wind blew the shingles off the barn and we had to ——— the chicken coops."

reckon – as in, "I don't care if it is an antique. You're not going to put that ——— this truck!"

recluse – as in, "With that, the inspector ——— me as to the importance of our mission and we goes on our way."

recommends – as in, "All right now, why were you boys trying to ——— restroom in the subway station?"

recompense – as in, "Chief say, this not dignified. White man slide down rock, ———."

reconcile – as in, "Yes, he——— marry him if he jsut holds out long enough."

rectangled – as in, "Your wife looked like a ——— all up in that fishing line."

rectify – as in, "Her career won't be ——— tell them that she spent last night with me!"

rector – as in, "Mary fell into the hog pen and ——— dress."

rectum – as in, "———? Hell, it killed'em."

recuperate – to rebuild chicken coops.

red – as in, "I ——— that book last year."

red fir – as in, "What did you hit ———?"

red-breasted – afflicted with a condition brought on by topless dancing in a chilly wind.

red-hot – as in, "She called him a lowdown, dirty, thieving pole-cat, and that's what made ———. He said he wasn't dirty!"

redolent – as in, "No, the car's not here. ——— it to Mr. Jones this morning."

reduce – as in, "Mother says that if we go to bed now she'll ——— a story."

reed – as in, "The sign says, no smoking. Can't you ——— ?"

reed organ – as in, "I can read piano music but I can't ———."

refer – as in, "Now Paw says he don't want us to scrape the hide off this bear because we won't be able to ——— it."

refuge – as in, "If you hadn't hollered at the ——— still be in the game!"

regency – as in, "I don't need any help with my territory. You just go back to the home office and tell them this is my ———."

regiment – as in, "I wonder what ——— by that last remark?"

region – as in, "Naw, they don't bite. Just ——— and grab one."

regulate – as in, "Hey, ——— man. What happened?"

rehearse – moving a corpse to another vehicle.

reign – as in, "It looks like it might ———. "

reins – as in, "We still hadn't completed the house when the ——— came."

relax – to take another laxative.

relay – to make love a second time.

relent – having loaned something for the second time.

render – as in, "The Missus ain't here, Sir. I ——— down to the store."

repair – as in, "I'm just waiting for the Grim ——— now."

require – to form a new vocal group for the church.

resent – as in, "Miss Murphy, this package will have to be ———."

resort – as in, "What a mess! Now we've got to ——— all this stuff."

rest on one's oars – to let a string of hookers support you.

retail – as in, "Yeah, Paw, it was awful. The mule backed into the propeller. Now, how are we gonna ——— her?"

reticent – as in, "Well, you really picked the wrong guy to stick up. I don't have a ———."

revenue – as in, "You should never ——— engine up like that."

reverend – to feel religiously strong about your girlfriend's posterior.

revival – as in, "Joe and Fred are okay now but we can't ———."

rhesus – as in, "I hope that this letter ——— you by Christmas."

rheumatic – an automatic room.

rhodium – a girl's name. Also, as in, "I ——— 'til he dropped."

ribald – as in, " Let's go down to the club and ——— Smedley."

ribbon – as in, "Who in blazes put this ——— my plate?"

rice – as in, "His Honor, Judge Junky. Everbody please ———. "

rickshaw – used to be a football player down at the high school.

righteous – as in, "Come on, Killer, one more ——— will have the match won."

rigor – as in, "Okay, I'll ——— to blow in exactly five minutes."

riot – as in, "Just ———, you'll like it."

ripper, – as in, "How on earth did Suzie ——— new frock?"

ritual – as in, "I reckon I could have ———, but I ain't much good at letter writin'."

roast – as in, "With these words he ——— to his full height of three and a half feet and tried to look stern."

robot – as in, "I think that I'll take the boat out and ——— five miles before dinner."

robust – as in, "Why did ——— my new bike?"

rockaway – as in, "Hey, man, you'd better throw that ———."

rocket – as in, "That dance hall is really gonna jump. Yep, we're really gonna ——— tonight."

rodeo – as in, "I couldn't find a horse so I ——— cow into town."

Roentgen – as in, "You've gambled all night and lost all our money! Is the ——— too?"

roll call – hollering up to the house to see if the biscuits are ready.

roly-poly – to mug a polar bear.

Roman – as in, "We've got to get this boat out of here. Stop talking and ———."

root stock – as in, "Mommy, I just heard a voice when I was playing around the apple tree. Do ——— ?"

roseate – as in, "There's no more food in the house. ——— everything in sight."

rosemary – as in, "Why did ——— that drummer?"

rosewood – as in, "Sarah might not, but ———."

rote – as in, "That was when I sat down and ——— you this here letter."

rotter – as in, "If that child keeps eating candy she's going to ——— teeth right out."

roughage – as in, "Seventeen is kind of a ———."

roulette – something you take for an acid stomach.

rounder – as in, "I can't help it. I just feel silly when I'm a———."

roundup – as in, "You'd better get that ———— , Bartender, or we're all leaving."

routine – an adolescent with bad manners.

royal – as in, "Come on, I want to introduce you to ————."

rubber – as in, "When my wife's not feeling good I ———— back."

rubble – as in, "A little ———— do you good."

ruble – as in, "I told you not to get that farm boy mad. If you fight him that ———— knock you silly."

ruby – as in, "After that this ———— pulls out a bowie knife and chases poor old Tom right out of town."

ruffian – one who makes ruffles.

ruler – as in, "Boys, either you follow this ———— I'm gonna kick ya out of town."

rumor – as in, "Did you find your ———— comfortable last night Mr. Merkley?"

rumpus – as in, "If the coach ever again kicks you in the ———— guys are gonna quit the the team."

rupture – as in, "Did you feel better after Linda ———— back?"

Russian – as in, "Stop ———— around and listen to me!"

rustle – as in, "If you spray your car with this stuff the ———— all be gone by tomorrow."

rusty – as in, "If it weren't for the ———— might get that old engine to run."

rutty – as in, "My husband's in a ———— just comes home and flops on the couch now."

rye – as in, "I know you don't like me, Estelle, but you could ————."

217

S

saber – as in, "I just want to sit here and ———— this moment."

sable – as the cow said, "Whatta ya ————. Let's go down to the pasture and kick up our heels."

saddle – as in, "If this movie's too ———— take you out for a soda."

Sadducee – as in, "I just can't help crying. This whole thing has made me very ————?"

safari – as in, "Well, ———— so good."

safety – as in, "I don't know what went wrong on your last two drives, Will. Here use this green one. It should be a ————."

sagely – as in, "Hey, don't put in so much ————."

Sahara – as in, "I thought I just ———— going into the ladies' room."

sail – something you attend after Christmas.

sailmaker – a department store.

sailor – as in "Is this aeolipile on ———— is this the regular price?"

saki – as in, "O.K., Yank, maybe you likee I give you ———— right in nose."

salamander – used to have a hotdog stand right across the street from the high school.

saleslady – as in, "This boat don't have an engine, we use ————."

saliva – as in, "When a horse lies down like that, there's one thing certain. Either it——— it ain't."

sallow – as in, "Be a good girl Lulu and ———— to the nice lady."

salmon – as in, "He couldn't have done it, Officer. I just saw ———— 25th Street, going into a laundromat."

salon – as in, "What I want to know is, is ——— my side, or is he going with you?"

salted – as in, "Please pass the ———."

saltpetre – as in, "How'd you ever get to be a cook's helper? That's way too much ———."

salutary – as in, "My friend, it seems we must split up. I'll go with ——— here and wait for the maiden."

Samoan – as in, "Are you sure he's dead? I just thought I heard ———."

sampan – as in, "I know he's the theater critic, but if he's also your best friend, why did ——— our opening? "

sample – as in, "We're not getting anywhere with this campaign. You've got to talk to him and make ——— his own weight around here."

Samson – as in, "Oh, so you're a girl. I thought you were ———."

sanctity – as in, "No, so far he hasn't sunk a putt, but on the last drive he ———."

sandal – as in, "Did you ——— these chairs before you painted them?"

sandalwood – as in, "No, to ——— take several days."

sandblast – as in, "Here comes that truckload of ——— him! Why couldn't he have shown up when he was supposed to."

sand dollar – as in, "Let's see, we could make a sand castle, or a sand dog, or a ——— whatever you want."

sandwich – as in, "Junior doesn't need a sandbox. He can play in that ——— the construction crew dumped in the backyard."

sandy – as in, "If we clean off some of that ——— may look pretty good."

sappy – as in, "Tell that ——— can pick up his things. He's fired!"

sapsucker – a confection made from the vital fluids of plants.

sari – as in, "I'm ——— you feel that way, Myrtle. My first three wives loved it!"

sarong – as in, "No, that's ——— I haven't had a drink for nearly ten minutes now."

satellite – as in, "Yes, it was very dark in the tunnel, and I had to grope my way along carefully. Then, as I turned a corner, there ———."

satiate – as in, "That woman has the biggest appetite I've ever seen. They ——— a whole pig at one sitting last year!"

satin – as in, "As I ——— my bath I suddenly realized that one of my toes was missing."

saturate – as in, "I finally gave up looking for them, but when I got home, there ——— pups on the front porch."

saturnine – as in, "When she opened the door, there ——— husbands."

sauce – tools for cutting boards.

saucer – as in, "You are the most impossible person I ever ———."

saurian – as in, "I'm really ——— I'll try to help if I can."

sausage – as in, "There's so much boozing going on these days that sometimes I think that we must be in the ———."

savor – as in, "Help, Sir Knight. My daughter has been carried off by a dragon. Please ———."

savory – as in, "When he found out he couldn't ——— ran screaming off into the woods."

sawyer – as in, "I ——— daughter out back of the barn with the hired man."

sax – as in, "Let's fill these ——— full of water and drop them out the window on people." Also, in Texas, refers to gender.

Saxon – as in, "Oh my God! Young Smedley left his ———— the bus."

Saxony – as in, "Then, he grabbed my ———— played one of the worst jazz choruses I've ever heard."

saxophone – as in, "Well, my Dear. If you intend to make a living off of ———— is absolutely necessary."

scabbard – in Old England, a nonunion minstrel.

scald – as in, "Hey Joe, there's some girl that———— about five times while you were out."

scallop – to remove one's hair forcibly with a knife.

scandal – as in, "I ———— the papers and there doesn't seem to be any mention of a robbery last night."

scandalize – as in, "The real ———— in her parents trying to make her give up the child."

scanty – a rundown, or poorly built shack or cabin.

scar – as in, "I saw his ———— parked in front of her house at three a.m."

scarab – a cross between a scoundrel and an Arab.

scarce – as in, "It is his indifference which really ———— me."

scarcity – a condition which might throw Britain into a panic.

scarify, – as in, "Pardon me Miss, ———— sit next to you?"

scarlet – as in, "Although it modified his looks, the ———— everyone know that he was a swordsman."

scary, – as in, "We gave him such a ———— never returned."

scatter – one who sings meaningless vocal sounds.

scene – as in, "That was the stupidest thing I've ever ————."

scenery – as in, "The teacher couldn't have ———— would have called the principal by now."

scenic – as in, "Hey, did you ———— down at the docks?"

scent – as in, "Why have you ——— me this miserable little gift, you cur?"

scepter – as in, "Yep, all the girls have already been taken ———."

scholarly – as in, "I can see by this report card that you're not much of a ———."

school – as in, "Don't eat that bowl of soup, Goldilocks, that's ———."

schoolmaster – as in, "Wait awhile before you go into the house. Your father is most upset with you for setting fire to the ———."

shottische – as in, "And then he went completely mad, grabbed a gun and ——— best hog."

scion – a hill in Jerusalem.

scissor – as in, "Was that your ——— or your cousin that I saw you with?"

scoff – as in, "Yes, Doctor. His ——— is much better this morning."

scold – as in, "Wow, it's ——— in here."

scone – as in, "He ——— get it when Paw gets back."

scorn – as in, "Whose ——— is that growing just south of your place?"

scorpion – as in, "El Presidente has sent me to ask you, how did you achieve such a ———?"

scot-free – as in, "Well, if he's not in the jail then I guess he's ———."

Scottish – as in, "He's ——— nerve, asking me to do that when I hardly know him."

scour – as in, "And, so saying, he whisk——— heroine away in his black limousine."

scramble – what you might say to avoid being gored.

scrappy – as in, "And from this miserable —— made a coat."

scream – as in, "Would you like some I ——?"

screw – as in, "This —— doesn't know a jib boom from a poop deck."

scribble – as in, "This —— never do. The baby's fallen out three times already!"

script, – as in, "I will never allow dear Uncle Peter to be buried in this ——."

scripture – as in, "I'll bet the gold is in this —— grandfather is buried in."

scrubby – to wash a honey-producing insect.

scruple – as in, "I'm afraid this —— be too loud for our Christmas dance."

scrutinize – as in, "You should never have —— girl like that!"

scullery – as in, "He must have taken a blow to the —— wouldn't be acting like that."

sculpture – as in, "Help, help, the Indians have —— Cousin Willy."

scum – as in, "This is the preacher, Dear. He's —— to ask you for your hand."

scurry – as in, "This —— is hot enough to take your head off!"

scurvy – as in, "Watch out for this road. It's ——."

scuttlebutt – to sink your rear.

scythe – as in, "She jutht thits around and —— all day."

seaboard – to find the ocean dull and unexciting.

seagoing – as in, "Where on earth is ——?"

sea horse – hookers on cruise ships.

seal – as in, "Yes, my Lad, the —— get to you after awhile."

sealed – run over by a seal.

sea lion – as in, "I love to see the ——— peaceful and calm like this."

sealskin – relatives of a seal.

seam – as in, "It would ——— so."

sea otter – as in, "A few years at ——— fix you, my Lad!"

seaport – a wine drunk on ocean-going vessels.

sear, – as in, "This ——— fellow says he's your long lost cousin."

seashore – as in, "I'm sorry, Mizz Purdy, but the Sheriff says we gotta ——— property,"

seaside – as in, "If it wasn't for these ——— probably be getting hungry."

season – – as in, "What ever made you want to go to ———?"

seasonable – to pour spices upon a male bovine animal.

seaward – as in, "Did you ——— down at the pool hall?"

secede – as in, "Our crop can't be a total failure. I ——— popping up here and there."

second hand – applause which comes after the first one.

secrete – as in, "I want to see Greece, Gilbraltar, and I want to ———."

sect – as in, "I ——— my hound dog on him."

secure – as in "Here, just swallow this. It's ——— for what ails you."

sedate – as in, "Whose ——— is that blonde girl over by the bar?"

sedge – as in, "He ——— you wouldn't like it very much."

sediment – as in, "She ——— to pick her up, but he never showed."

seduce – as in, "I ——— damn bicycle was that in the driveway?"

sedum – as in, "I ——— both at the dance last night."

seersucker – one who falls for a phony clairvoyant.

seesaw – as in, "We've got to make sure we ——— the evidence this time."

seine – as in, "I don't think he is quite ———."

seize – as in, "He says ——— indisposed right now."

seizure – as in, "Once you've sailed the ——— never quite the same."

seldom – as in, "I think that you ——— products at this store!"

selfish – as in, "I never thought that I would ——— for a living."

seller – another word for basement.

Seltzer – as in, "They should get along all right unless he in———."

semaphore – as in, "I usually grade papers from one to five. Some of these papers received two's and three's and I gave ———."

semi – as in, "——— threw away, and ——— kept."

seminar – as in, "You don't have to go out for kindling, there's ——— woodbox."

Semite – as in, "Yes, ——— but I never would!"

senate – as in, "I can't understand your not receiving it. I——— by mail to you last month."

Senegalese – as in, "Why, Dudley, would you ——— crumby little flowers?"

senhor – as in, "Hey, Mert, I just ——— wife drinking with the barber down at Murphy's saloon."

sensual – as in, "He ——— his best wishes!"

sensuous – as in, "I guess Mommy got tired of us, Daddy, or else why would she ———."

sentence – as in, "Our boys on the front lines have nowhere to sleep. We've got to ———."

sentinel – as in, "I got a call for a girl to pop naked, out of a cake while you were gone. Sarah wouldn't do it so I ———."

sequel – to look for a fountain of water.

sequence – as in, "I ———— he comes and where he goes." (Biblical)

serenade – used to be a cheerleader down at the high school.

serf – a line of foamy water where the sea breaks upon the shore.

series – as in, "Yes, ———— right outside your door."

serpent – one of King Arthur's lesser knights.

serpentine – an adolescent snake.

serum – as in, "Throw these steaks in the pan and ————."

service – as in, "To ———— my greatest pleasure, Sir!"

serviette – as in, "Sorry I'm late for our tennis match. Did you ————?"

servile – knight who undid Arthur's court.

settee – as in, "'I'm a man of very few words',————."

setter – as in, "Just ———— down over there boys."

settle – as in, "We've got to get a new TV. This old———— never work."

sewer – as in, "If she gives you any trouble, ————."

shackle – as in, "You call this a house? This ———— fall apart the first time it snows."

Shakespeare – an act performed by armed, native hostiles.

shamble – a cow with a ring in its nose.

shampoo – a character trying to pass himself off as A.A. Milne's favorite bear.

shamrock – what they use in some outdoor movie scenes.

shanty – as in, "The King shall be here soon, ———— ?"

share – singer who used to be Mrs. Bono.

shavetail – a story about your losing your beard.

shawl – as in, "We Iranians know that the ——— never be deposed."

shears – as in, "And this is the lady who ——— my life."

sheep – inexpensive.

sheeepshead – as in, "At this time of day, the barn is where the ———."

sheepskin – the relatives of a sheep.

sheer – as in, "This sounds fantastic. Are you ———?"

shekel – as in, "I think I'll get up and ——— the doors and windows."

Shekinah – as in, "——— reminds me of my late wife."

shelter – as in, "Yes, Sir, we ——— for three days, and we still had a lot of resistance when we attacked."

Sheraton – to possess 2,000 pounds in conjunction with others.

sherbet – a wager made with no possibility of losing.

sherry – as in, "His stocks are really worth something now. For one ——— got over $500 yesterday."

shinny – as in, "After kicking my ——— began pummeling me with his fists."

Shinto – as in, "And then she kicked my ———."

shipshape – to have a body which is built like a seagoing vessel.

shoal – as in, "Ah ——— try to do that sah."

shoe – as in, "Is that ——— Bert?"

shoe horn – something you wear when walking in traffic.

shogun – as in, "No, I never shoot this revolver. This is only a ———."

shoot off one's mouth – an accident caused by brushing your teeth with gunpowder.

shoot off one's mouth

shooting star – a way to elevate the understudy.

shoplifter – a huge forklift.

shore – as in, "I ——— hope this changes your luck!"

shortbread – having very little money on hand.

short change – to put on another costume quickly.

short circuit – to have only two gigs during the year.

shorten – as in, "No, you gave me sixty bucks, so I'm still ———."

shorthand – a birth defect.

shortsighted – as in, "The guys who borrowed my ——— him over on Main Street."

shoulder – as in, "Yesh, I ——— my wife'sh fur coat!"

shovel – as in, "I think that one ——— start this boulder down the hill now."

shrewd – to be attacked by shrews.

shriek – a desert chieftain.

shutter – as in, "This should ——— up."

Siamese – as in, "Excuse me, Sir, would you ——— checks before you leave?"

sickle – as in, "Without this serum the ——— never recover."

side – as in, "I guess I'm just doomed to a life of loneliness, she ———."

sidearms – the position in which most people find their upper appendages.

sideboard – as in, "I think that it was the half-time advantage of 94 to nothing which made our ———."

sideshow – as in, "Louise, take a look at where I've torn my dress. Does my ———?"

sierra – as in, "Oh, I ——— drinking man, McTavish."

sigh – a man's name.

sighted – as in, "Did I hear you just ———?"

sign – as in, "Oh, stop your ——— get back to work."

signature – as in, "What is the meaning of the ——— king wears on his ring?"

Sikh – as in, "Not tonight, George! I'm feeling rather ———."

silence – as in, "No wonder he doesn't have any tools ——— out everything he owns!"

silently – as in, "As a matter of fact, ——— his wife just last week."

silhouette – as in, "I want you to take a look at this window and see what made the ———."

silicon – as in, "And then last week he tried to escape by dressing up like the warden's mother-in-law. He's really a ———."

silk stocking – to increase one's silk.

silky – the key you keep under the window sill.

silly – as in, "When his fingers slipped off the ——— fell fourteen floors and landed in a Banyan tree."

silo – as in, "I think that it was losing all his money on chicken-gizzard futures that's made ———."

silvery – as in, "I don't know what happened, Sir. After he saw all of that ——— just kind of went mad."

simulate – as in, "Hey ———. The meeting's already started."

since – as in, "For these ——— you must do penitence, my son."

sincere – as in, "Why should we travel any further, ——— we have everything we need?"

sine – as in, "Would you just ——— here, Sir?"

sinecure – as in, "Well, Sweetheart. I always say that it takes one ——— another."

sinew – as in, "But after your original —— went on to many others."

sinewy – as the Louisiana courts told Mr. Long, "That's a ——."

single – as in, "When he heard the beautiful melodies issuing from Jonathan Livingston's throat, he was forced to shout, 'Oh ——!'"

single file – as in, "Just look at my tool box since he used it. There's not one —— left."

single-breasted – a birth defect.

single-handed – a birth defect.

Sing Sing – a school of vocal music in New York State.

sinister – as in, "My —— love, not wisely, but too well."

sink – as in, "I —— you'd better leave now."

sinker – as in, "Let's put a round below her water line, Mr. Travis, and see if we can ——."

sinuate – as in, "When we said we were going to write down our very worst sin, I wrote mine on a fortune cookie. That was my ——."

sinus – as in, "I think that the audition went great, but are they going to ——?"

Sirius – as in, "What? You can't be ——."

sirloin – one of King Arthur's knights.

Sisal – as in, "Maw says you can wait in the parlor. My —— be down in a minute."

sissy – as in, "John —— doesn't want to go now."

sister – as in, "I'll go over and see if I can a——."

sistine – a teenage sister.

site – as in, "Oh what a —— he was."

six – as in, "Every time I go past his house he —— his mutt on me."

size – as in, "I couldn't stand his ———, so I put a muzzle on him."

skedaddle – as in, "Don't you have any whisk——— warm a man's insides?"

skeleton key – the pitch at which a skeleton feels most comfortable singing.

skeptic – a tank for disposing of waste matter.

skerry – as in, "It gave him such a ——— took off running and has never been seen since."

sketch – as in, "Whose ——— is that floating around in the bay?"

skid – as in, "Whose ——— is this?"

skier – as in, "Whooee, Boy, you really gimme a ———."

skiff – as in, "I just want to a——— Joannie can go tonight."

skin – as in, "Whose ——— is that in the picture over the mantel?"

skinflint – used to produce a spark by striking a flint against the external covering.

skinny – as in, "After he shed his ——— slithered away into the bushes."

skipjack – as in, "No, let's ———. He's extremely dull at parties."

skipper – as in, "He didn't like Flossie, so everytime he came to her name on the list, he used to ———."

sky – as in, "Get him out of here! This ——— is driving me nuts."

slack – as in, "Looks ——— we ain't gonna be goin' home yet!"

slap – as in, "So saying, she proceeded to sit in his ———."

sled – as in, "Yes, the President's speech has ——— to quite a bit of confusion."

sleigh – as in, "I must go out and ——— the dragon before that ridiculous Saint George bags them all."

slime – as in, "Who put this ——— in my drink?"

slipper – as in, "Let's ——— a mickey and get rid of her."

slip up – as in, "For heaven's sake, Daughter. Never pull your —— in public."

slobber – as in, "Either he's a —— there's been a herd of buffalos living in this place."

slogan – a weapon with a very low velocity.

sloppy – as in, "If the prince sees this —— will execute every cook in the palace!"

slough – as in, "Yes, that's —— and Grandpa Nuttely in that picture."

Slovak – a vacuum cleaner which doesn't work very well.

slumber – as in, "Where did you get all of this ——?"

slurry – a county in Southeastern England.

smacker – as in, "If little Eva gives you any trouble, ——."

small arms – something found on the upper bodies of children.

smarty – as in, "He's so —— just lost our entire fortune in the stock market."

smelter – as in, "I knew she was here. I —— the minute I entered the room."

smiles – as in, "Why has —— been so standish offish?"

smite – as in, "His folks will never lend them any money, but hers ——."

Smithsonian – as in, "We tried —— my Zenith portable and we still couldn't get a picture."

smitten – a small mitten.

smoulder – a smooth boulder.

smother – as in, "Whose —— has to give the Girl Scout tea this year?"

smuggle – as in, "If we don't bump him off this —— spill everything to the cops."

smutty – as in, "After that rain it really is ———— out there."

snapper – as in, "Go into the bedroom. Your sister wants you to ———— up."

sneer – as in, "Since we've been going together, I can always tell when she's ————."

sneeze – as in, "He looks ridiculous in short pants since his ———— are very knobby."

snooze – as in, "I find this ———— very disturbing."

snowball – making love outdoors in the winter.

snowbush – as in, "That's ————, that's a damned tree!"

snow owl – as in, "Run! That's ————, it's Dracula."

snuffbox – a bout of pugilism to decide who gets the powdered tobacco.

snuffle – as in, "Get rid of that stuff. That ———— ruin your nostrils."

soapy – as in, "Reaching for the ———— lost his balance and fell, naked through the large window."

social – as in, "And ———— it always be."

socialize – untruths which you tell at gatherings.

socket – as in, "If this stupid dummy won't stand up I'm gonna ————."

soda – as in, "Mr. Merkle, I ———— new button on your shirt."

sodden – as in, "With this he lay down upon the ———— began crying and beating his fists."

Sodomite – as in, "I think you're overworking your lawn. You ought to take it easy on that ————."

solace – as in, "I've got to go now, Estelle. ———— waiting for me at the delicatessen."

solar – as in, "We ———— house, and now we have no place to live."

solder – one who cuts sod.

soldier – as in, "Yes, I ——— dog while you were away because he kept dragging little kids into the backyard and trying to bury them."

sole – as in, "I do believe he has given his ——— to the devil."

solo – as in, "I never thought that you would stoop ——— Harry."

Solomon – as in, "And so, upon this ——— occasion, we are gathered here to pay tribute to the town drunk, old Fred."

sombre – a New England samba.

somersault – used to enhance the flavor of food during the warm months of the year.

sonata – as in, "It's getting ——— single day goes by without one of you dummies being suspended for afterhours violations."

sonnet – as in, "I know that's my breakfast tray, Harriet, but what's ———?"

soon – as in, "I don't care whether the company wants to give in now! I'm ——— them anyway!"

sorcerer – as in, "Tell me, what is the ——— information?"

sore – as in, "His arrows would ——— for miles, often coming down in surprising and unexpected places."

sorghum – what you have after the dentist pulls a tooth.

sorrel – as in, "If you keep picking it that ——— never heal!"

souffle – as in, "Why did ——— her husband with his buggy whip?"

soul – as in, "Going, going, gone. ——— to the highest bidder."

sounding board – as in, "I think that you need a vacation, Dear. You've been ——— lately."

sour – as in, "He says he ——— daughter going into the woods with Tom McIver's boy."

source – as in, "I don't know what happened, Doc. I kept getting these ———, and the next thing I knew, my ears fell off."

souse – female pigs.

soviet – as in, "I'll never invite them to dinner again. Aunt ——— up just about everything in sight."

sower – as in, "I don't know what we did last night, but I sure do feel ———."

soya – as in, "I ——— at Miz Grundy's dancing school last week."

space – as in, "Yep, the vet says that he ——— about 200 animals a month."

spade – as in, "Yep, first the corn crop failed; then the barn burned down. My oldest boy ran over my prize rooster with the tractor; and to top it all, while my wife was in the hospital to have her tonsils out, some idiot doctor ——— her instead."

sparkle – as in, "Don't touch that wire while the motor's running. The ——— knock you flat!"

sparrow – a row of plants that you didn't actually have to plant.

sparse – as in, "He must really want to win this fight. He ——— for hours every day."

spatula – as in, "I don't want to argue. If this is going to be a ——— have to excuse me."

specialize – as in, "I know it's wrong to tell the children that there is a Santa Claus and an Easter Bunny but these are very ———."

specialty – as in, "Here, try this Darjeeling blend. It's a very ———."

speechless – as in, "The President does talk strangely. As I hear him more I begin to like his ———."

speedster – to mix something very fast.

spencer – as in, "How much money did you ———?"

spice – enemy agents.

spider – as in, "Just then I looked down the block and —— going into a massage parlor."

spider monkey – as in, "I —— sitting on top of the chandelier."

spindle – as in, "I work and slave all day long and what do you do? You go out and —— my money on junk like this."

spine – as in, "This —— tree is rotten."

spinet – as in, "Look, Buster, why don't you just take your top and ——?"

spinster – man who operates a roulette wheel.

spiral – as in, "If you design the church steeple like that the —— come off in the first high wind!"

spiritual – a southern expression, as in, "That's the ——."

spiritualize – as in, "He may be worldly, but he has the most ——."

spittoon – a melody which is perfect for expectorating.

splay – as in, "Let's leave. This —— is obscene!"

sponsor – as in, "It is in these headwaters that the female salmon —— eggs."

spoonbill – what the restaurant makes you pay for wrecking the tableware.

spoor – as in, "This —— sap didn't even know he had done anything wrong."

sporty – as in, "So, like a good —— agreed to share part of my money with me."

spot – as in, "This —— hasn't got a high in a carload."

spread-eagle – as in, "I'm trying to clean the house. Meanwhile, your damned bird continues to —— droppings all over the place."

spreader – as in, "She was fine on the honeymoon, but afterwards she commenced to —— clothes all over the house."

springbok – what a rookie pitcher does in training camp that costs his team a man on first base.

spurious – as in, "I know we're only horses, but if these guys continue to ——— like this let's dump them off."

sputter – as in, "With this, he bent his ——— into a bow and flung it through the clubhouse window."

spy – as in, "This——— is different. I baked it with my new blow dryer."

squadron – as in, "And then, just for laughs, the sergeant used to ride in his jeep and make the rest of the ———."

square – as in, "A——— he got that ice cream cone."

stable – a command to keep the animal from moving.

stagnate – as in, "Did you come to the dance ———?"

stain – as in, "Where are you ——— here in town?"

stair – as in, "When I saw his clothing, or rather the lack of it, I was forced to ———."

stake–as in, "And for dinner, Count Dracula, how about a——?"

stalagmite – as in, "A stalac never would, but a ———."

stale – as in, "I hope that your ——— be a pleasant one."

stalwart – a small, hard, abnormal growth caused by cleaning out a horse barn.

stance – as in, "No, this isn't Art's, it's ———."

stand pat – as in, "If she tries to go along with this Watergate thing, I'm going to ——— on her head."

stanza – as in, "I think that ——— really rotten guy."

starry – as in, "While standing outside gazing at the ——— was mugged by a passing girl scout."

startle – as in, "This——— really kick off our benefit this year."

state – as in, "Yes, Sir, the murderer ——— at our house for weeks."

stately – as in, "No, you now owe over 6,000 dollars to the
———."

steelworks – as in, "Whatever gave you the idea to ——— of art?"

steerage – as in, "Yes, when this country was young, the
people didn't eat nearly as much beef. But, we've now come
into the ———."

stickleback – as in, "Don't worry about the mob. The big guy
with the ——— you up if you speak."

sticky – as in, "As he picked up the ——— was suddenly overrun by a crazed corsortium of puppy dogs."

stiffen – as in, "Let's bury this ——— get outta here. This place
gives me the willies."

stile – as in, "Well, at least he has ———."

stirrup – as in, "Well, you've managed to ——— quite a hornet's
nest." Also something you put on your pancakes.

stocking – placing people in the stocks.

stockpot – the normal, everyday type of marijuana.

stoneware – as in, "I found this ——— you left it, right in the
middle of the driveway."

stopcock – to call off your rooster.

story – as in, "The first time he came into the ——— bought a
six-pack of beer, and a copy of the Baghavad Gita."

straighten – as in, "When I said that, he went ——— to the
house and told his mother."

strawberry – as in, "Hay is all right, but I don't like ——— much."

stricture – as in, "Until they caught us in the parlor I didn't
realize how ——— parents are."

strikebreaker – someone who breaks your concentration
when you're bowling.

string bean – as in, "This is what I've been looking for. How
long has this ——— here?"

structure – as in, "Yes, Sir. I saw him when he ——— paw. That was his first and last mistake."

strumpet – a three-valve musical instrument, usually made of brass.

stubble – as in, "That's no good. if you cut it off the ——— still be there."

stucco – as in, "Oh, I'm ——— I'm ——— I'm ——— I'm stuck!"

student – an indentation in your car put there when your wife threw a bowl of stew at you as you were running out the back door.

studied – a mare after being mated.

stupefy – as in, "I wouldn't ——— had to! Someone else can pick the strawberries!"

Styx – as in, "——— and stones may break my bones . . . ."

subconsciousness – a unique quality exhibited frequently by Admirals in charge of fleet convoys.

subdue – as in, "I know we've got to get off this island quickly, but there's a ——— any minute now."

subhuman – a sailor who is on submarine duty.

sublet – as in, "We had that freighter right between us and then the other ——— him slip away."

sublime – what British submarine sailors use to prevent scurvy.

submission – the reason for taking your submarine out of port.

submit – as in, "Jawohl, Captain. Ve haf sighted an allied ——— der periscope."

subscribe – a person on submarines who writes letters for the illiterate members of the crew.

subserve – to have done duty on a submarine.

subside – as in, "Let's leave the ship on the side where the destroyers are moored, not on the ———."

subsist – a growth caused by submarine duty.

substance – a method of planting one's legs on a submarine deck, to keep from being thrown down when she dives.

succeed – a method of getting nourishment while not actually swallowing anything.

succor – a lollypop.

succumb – as in, "Hey, how's ——— you and Mary aren't going together anymore?"

suffer – as in, "We can't find a place to live in permanently, ——— the meantime we're just camping out here."

suffix – as in, "Tell that hophead that if he does the job there's ——— waiting for him."

sugar loaf – a lazy, lethargic condition caused by eating too much sugar.

suite – as in, "Come with me, my ———."

suitor – as in, "If this doesn't ——— tell her to come back again."

sulphur – as in, "Yes, we like it, but how much does a house like this ———?"

Sulu – as in, "You tell him that if he doesn't make a settlement with us by this afternoon we're going to ——— for everything he has."

sum – as in, "——— of these days, you're gonna miss me honey!"

sumach – as in, "And tell him we're gonna ——— too!"

Sumerian – as in, "We might even ——— Elizabeth for helping them!"

summary – as in, "My, this weather is ———."

summit – as in, "You can make up your own mind. ——— helps and ——— doesn't."

summon – as in, "If you want a toothpick there's ——— the table."

sunder – Sunday, as pronounced by a New Englander.

sundew – as in, "The moon don't give much light, but the ———."

sundial – as in, "He loves doing it, so once in a while I let my ——— the telephone."

sundown – as in, "Hey, Luke. I saw your ——— at the barber-shop getting himself all fixed up."

sunken – as in, "I've got more money ——— this place than you'll ever see."

sunny – as in, "Yes, we were going to leave this morning, but my ——— got bit by a rattler and we had to wait a day."

sunrise – as in, "That'll be the day when I see my ——— before noon."

sunset – as in, "I wish I could make my ——— down with the family just once in awhile. He's always running off with those no-good friends of his."

sunshine – as in, "I paid a dollar to have my ——— our car, and while he was in the house getting a drink somebody stole the hubcaps."

sunspot – as in, "What are you doing out here in the ———? You don't want to go into the house and be annoyed by those cats, do you boy?"

super – to feed her soup.

superb – used to be a cheerleader down at the high school.

supercargo – as in, "I hear that you're carrying a load of Las Vegas dancing girls, eh, Captain? That's a ———."

supercilious – very, very silly.

superficial – an official who does a really great job.

superhuman – as in, "She's just really a ———."

superinduce – as in, "As a union member, he's not too good. Although he is ———."

supernatural – an exaggerated, afro hair style.

supersaturate – as in, "Hey, Shirl. I hear that since you've been dating him, the ——— lower for the apartment."

superstructure – a great teacher.

suppose – elastic, support stockings.

surcease – a lesser known knight of King Arthur's.

surcharge – as in, "I'm sorry, but if you are a knight you have to pay ten percent more. There's a ——— for your title, you know."

sure – as in, "Okay, I'll just ——— to her room."

surety – as in, "This is not coffee. Is this ———?"

surmount – as in a knight addressing his steed, "Are you ready then ———?"

surpass – another of King Arthur's knights.

surplus – knight who was good at addition.

surrey – as in, "No, ———never told me to do that!"

surrogate – as in, "Yes, ——— blocks our path to the south end of the fortress, but our way lies clear to the north."

surround – a very fat knight at Arthur's court.

surtax – money paid for the privilege of being a knight.

surveillance – as in, "Here's everything you will need, ———, helmet, gauntlets, broad sword, chain mail, shield, etc."

suture – as in, "So you ——— doctor because he sewed you up with a transistor radio left inside you?"

swallowtail – as in, "Medicine Man say it all right to eat head of fish, but not good to ———."

swami – a Swedish mommy.

swan – as in, "Okay, Buster, this ——— is for you."

swarm – as in, "I say, it's ——— today, isn't it?"

swarthy – as in, "I ain't comin' out flatfoot. I ——— cops would never get me, and you never will!"

swatter – as in, "This ——— tastes like turpentine."

sweater – as in, "Let's throw her in the sauna and ———."

sweatshop – a place to buy a sweater.

Swede – as in, "That was certainly ——— of you."

sweetbread – as in, "Yeh, it's a lousy job, but I'm really making ———."

sweetish – a resident of Sweeten.

swelter – as in, "Gosh, Mona, you've really been ——— me."

swish – pertaining to a European country, known for its banks.

switchback – as in, "All right, kid, if you know what's good for you, you'll put that ———."

switchboard – something an unscrupulous lumber company might do when you're not looking. Also a dull, uninterested feeling primarily affecting telephone operators.

sword – as in, "His kite ——— over the rooftops."

swore – as in, "If you keep shooting at us this ——— is never going to end."

sycamore – as in, "You're lucky the witch doctor gave you that charm or you might have been ———."

syllable – as the cow said to her mate after he'd been cutting up, "Oh, you're such a ———."

symbol – an African word for lion.

symmetry – as in, "Well, we can't very well sell him an entire redwood, but we might lease ———."

symphony – as in, "Yeh, Marsha and I were getting along great until ——— guy gave her a big line about how rich he was. Now they're married, and she's supporting him."

syndicate – as in, "It would be a ——— these flowers! They're too beautiful!"

synonym – as in, "Oh no, Fred, we mustn't! Roger is my husband, and I would never ———."

syntax – something you pay to support the people's vices.

syphilis – Why don't you come to my party? ——— coming, and she's bringing her pet armadillo."

syrup – what you step into when you get upon a horse.

tabby – as in, "When the bartender showed him his ——— began to cry."

tablet – as in, "I don't know why ——— that girl make such a fool of him."

taboo – as in, "Yes, it was ——— first suggested that we join the Bobolink Club."

tacit – as in, "And then, your Honor, she picked up my copy of the *Kama Sutra,* and tried to ——— out the door."

tackle – as in, "This ——— make him get up out of his chair quickly!"

tact – as in, "We ——— back and forth for hours before we were able to round the point."

tactic – as in, "And then I told Richard, you just sat on a ———."

tactical – tickling someone with a tack.

tactile – as in, "If he doesn't address the preacher with some ——— take him home and beat him!"

tadpole – a Polish fellow named Thaddeus.

tabby

tail – as in, "I've heard many stories, but even for a hooker this is a very strange ———."

tailor – as in, "Look here, sailor, did you pay me for some ——— do you just want to talk?"

tailpiece – what you get in a brothel.

Taiping – a ping pong game in Thailand.

talebearer – the second man in the horse costume.

taleteller – one who informs your wife that she saw you coming out of a house of ill repute.

tamale – as in, "He didn't pay much attention to Martha, but he was very nice ———."

tambour – as in, "Please, Sir, don't ——— with my affections."

tandem – as in, "Upon hearing this nonsense, I grabbed those two kids, took them out into the woodshed and ———."

tangent – as in, "All I can tell you, Inspector, is that he was a real ———. He must have come from Southern Europe somewhere."

tangible – as in, "Oh, by the way, I ——— last week and you can pick up the hide anytime you like."

tangle – a South American dance.

tank – an expression of appreciation, as in, "——— you very much."

tankard – a ship which carries oil.

tannin – as in, "Within a moment we were overrun with Indians. I counted ——— they were still coming."

tansy – as in, "No, I'm not going to work this afternoon. I'm going to lie out here and get me a———?"

tantalate – as in, "The bizarre story of a woman who ——— husband's hide, and had it made into lamp shades."

tantamount – an operation performed by a cavalryman who preserved the hide of his late steed.

tantrum – as in, "No, not the white snare. I want to play that big ————."

taper – as in, "We had to ———— mouth shut to keep her from biting us."

tapestry – as in, "Yeh, Jones wants to get some maple syrup so we're going over and watch him ————."

tar – a Texas pronunciation, as in, "The ———— of Babel."

tarantella – an Italian game in which the participants rip each other's clothing and then announce to the assemblage which parts they have exposed.

tardy – as in, "Today I'm going to ———— roof."

target – as in, "How the hell did all of this ———— on the rug?"

tariff – as in, "Stand still! Your shirt is going to have a much larger ———— you keep pulling away."

tarpon – as in, "Who left this ———— my bed?"

tarry – a man's name.

tarsus – as in, "First he ————, and then he feathers us."

tart – as in, "Be careful where you walk. The driveway was just freshly ————."

tartan – as in, "I told you it was ———— you walked in it anyway."

Tartar – one who chases after tarts.

tatter – as in, "Her associations with men ———— the ways of the world at an early age."

tax – small, sharply pointed fastening devices.

taxi – as in, "Why don't you go sit on a ————."

tea – the twentieth letter of the alphabet.

tea house – as in, "After ———— about making out, Baby?"

team – as in, "I know he can't play, but the boss says we've got to get him some clubs, take him out, and ———— up anyway."

tease – what you put your golf ball upon.

technic – as in, "Rutgers? I thought you were going to Cal ———."

teeter – as in, "I think that I ——— off when I said that."

teetotaler – one who drinks nothing but tea.

temperance – as in, "First you heat 'em up red-hot, then you throw 'em into some ice water, and that's how you ———."

temperature – as in, "I'm surprised at how ——— climate is here."

temporal – as in, "You've got to watch your ———. I can't keep bailing you out of jail all the time."

tempter – as in, "I'll get some candy and ——— into my room."

tenancy – as in, "That little blonde doesn't look too expensive. Why don't you offer her a ———?"

tender – as in, "Und now chentlemen, for another ——— Fraulein will take it all off."

tenement – as in, "Until you've been really broke, you'll never know just how much that ———."

tenon – as in, "I'm gonna put a ——— double zeros and go for the big one this time."

tenpins – as in, "It's about time someone sewed up your pants. You have ——— holding them together."

tense – what you live in when you're out camping.

tensile – as in, "——— at least keep the rain off of you."

tensor – as in, "Sweetheart, are you ——— do you always stiffen up like this?"

tentacle – a five-sided, star-shaped tent.

tenure – as in, "Here's the ——— sister got from the milkman yesterday."

terminal – as in, "An 'A' in math this ——— be in good shape for graduation."

terminate – as in, "He finished his final exam of the ——— a huge chocolate sundae to celebrate."

termite – as in, "If I don't get my head straightened out, this ——— be my last here at old Potbelly 'U'."

terra cotta – a mixture of cottage cheese and earth.

terrain – as in, "Hmm, it looks like it's going ———."

terrible – something which tears easily.

terrier – as in, "He seemed like such a quiet guy; I never thought he would do something like ——— blouse."

terrify – as in, "——— tissue?"

territory – as in, "Yes, my name is Terence, and you can tell those Whigs that ——— is here."

terror – as in, "Is that a ———was your suit made with slits in it?"

terse – terrible verse.

testate – as in, "The ——— up so much time, students, that we will have to finish our discussion tomorrow."

testy – one half of the male reproductive organ.

Teuton – as in, "No, I haven't seen your father for three days. He must have a——— again."

Teutonic – as in, "No, that's the number ———. This mixture of castor oil and gin is our number one."

textile – ceramic squares manufactured in Texas.

texture – as in, "The Bishop would like to speak to the elders about the ——— pastor delivered last Sunday. He doesn't feel that 'Screwing Off' is a proper title for a sermon."

thaw – as in, "I thought I ——— a puddy tat."

thesis – abbreviation for "the sister."

thistle – as in, "We'll pass the ball to the tight end, who will pass it to the halfback, who will pass it to the fullback, who will pass it back to the quarterback and ——— really confuse 'em."

Thor – as in, "You think you're ———; I can hardly move!"

throne – as in, "So far in this game the quarterback has ——— 62 interceptions and has been sacked 37 times."

through – as in, "At this point, the quarterback fell back and ——— the ball straight up in the air."

thunderclap – applause for some of Jupiter's work.

thunderhead – a toilet with noisy plumbing.

thyme – as in, "——— after ——— I tell myself that Y'me so lucky to be loving you!"

thyroid – a shy, lisping android.

ticket – as in, "You shouldn't ——— so lightly."

tickle – as in, "This ——— back out just as soon as I apply a little heat to his rear."

tidal – as in, "I ——— the girls clothes in knots. Let's see what happens when they come out of the water."

tide – as in, "With this score we have ——— last years record of one win and thirteen losses."

tiding – floating around in the tide.

tidy – an area with extremes in tides.

tie – a resident of Thailand.

tier – as in, "Upon hearing this news she shed a little ———."

tiger – one who ties things.

tile – as in, "This red ——— never go with that yellow and blue checked suit."

tiller – as in, "I'm going to wait ——— new boyfriend dumps her, and then I'll just move back in."

time – a spice.

timely – as in, "I'd love to but we just don't have ———."

timepiece – as in, "It's about —— was declared. This war has lasted over a hundred years, and besides, we're running out of roses."

tinned – as in, "After much use the pages —— to curl up at the edges."

tinsel – as in, "What on earth would make —— so high this month?"

tiny – to bind up one's leg joint between the thigh and ankle.

tipple – as in, "A little —— make her happier."

tipsy – as in, "You bums had better leave me a ——, or next time I'll dump your soup on ya!"

tire – as in, "Here, —— up with this light cord."

tissue – as in, "Ah, my Lord, ——, 'tis really you."

Titan – as in, "You'd better tie her up really —— watch out for her teeth, she bites!"

tithe – as in, "Yeth, thih —— our all-time club record!"

title – as in, "Getting too —— make you do silly things."

toad – as in, "He was terrible last semester, but since then he's —— the line pretty well."

toadstool – a handy place for a toad to sit down.

toaster – to tickle a woman with your toes.

toastmaster – as in, "It is I, Igor. I have brought your breakfast ——."

toddle – as in, "Little —— show you where your bedroom is."

toiler – a New England toilet.

Tokay – as in, "Hey, how's about giving me a little ——."

token – as in, "Ah —— he cain't come around here anymore!"

"Just what we need, tolerance!"

tolerance – as in, "Do you mean to tell me that you've spent three years and six million dollars of the institute's money trying to increase the height of insects? Just what we need, ———."

toll – as in, "Ah ——— you before, no more free handouts."

Toltec – an ancient Mexican technical school.

tomahawk – as in, "Yes, I bought the twins a pair of carrier pigeons for Christmas, and just for fun, I bought ———."

tomfool – as in, "Why would Uncle ——— around with a woman like that?"

tone – as in, "The coast guard cutter just radioed that they're ——— the yacht back into port."

tongue-tied – an operation which was performed on someone with an extremely long tongue.

tonight – as in, "And so, as your Queen, it is my privilege ——— you."

tool – as in, "No, never mind bringing all of them. ——— be enough."

tootle – as in, "It won't take much more for me to leave George. One more good ——— do it."

topic – your first round draft choice.

topless – as in, "It's a shame to have lost his toys. He misses his bear, I know, although I think he misses his ———."

topple – as in, "My ——— beat your old top any time."

topsoil – as in, "This new synthetic lubricant will last for the life of the engine, and that ———."

torment – as in, "Until you have to live in an open barrack with about fifty other guys you never know how much a ———."

tornado – as in, "It was the lack of definitive leadership, plus the increasing communist influence in member countries which really ——— apart."

torso – as in, "They ——— many goal posts down last year that we had to increase the athletic department's budget."

torture – as in, "I ate that ——— sister made and felt sick for three days afterward!"

totem – as in, "Take these buckets of water and ——— up to the house."

toucan – as in the old quotation, "——— live as cheaply as one!"

toupee – as in, "Yes, he likes to play around, but when the bills come due he doesn't want ———."

tour – "——— all right, I guess, but three kids would be too much."

towhead – to move a portable toilet from one place to another by means of a rope attached to a vehicle.

toxin – as in, "No, we're safe so long as he ——— circles like he usually does. But if the professor ever starts being coherent, watch out: trouble."

trace – what you get breakfast in bed on.

tracer – as in, "If you're finished, may I have your ———?"

tractor – as in, "We could sell them this ——— perhaps that acreage down by the lake would appeal to them."

trader – as in, "I'd like to take my wife down and ——— for a pickup truck."

trade school – as in, "Sure, I'd ——— for a job any day."

Trappist – one who makes a living trapping animals.

trapshooting – a gambling game played with two die or dice.

treason – as George Washington's father is supposed to have said, "Did you chop down this ———?"

treaty – a warm beverage made from the bark of the eucalyptus.

tremor – as in, "The edges of the lawn are looking really shaggy. I'd better get out the ———."

trestle – as in, "This little ——— really make me the life of the party! It's topless, backless and bottomless. Actually, it's a belt."

triad – an initial experiment in selling something.

triangular – someone who plays a triangle.

trickle – as in, "This ——— really blow their minds."

trinket – as in, "I don't care how bad it smells. ———."

triple – as in, "Hey, you should be in Hollywood. The ——— do you good!"

triplet – as in, "Listen, this girl is so dumb that she once, on a ——— some guy she'd just met carry her suitcase for her and never saw either of them again!"

tripod – as in, "If alcohol gets you down, ———."

tripoli – as in, "All right, son, I want a straight answer because he might have been seriously hurt. Why did you ———?"

trite – as in, "I ——— and ———, but I couldn't quite reach the cord to turn off the light!" (anonymous)

troll – as in, "You have a very ——— sense of humor."

trollop – one who rides the trolley car.

trombone – a short vertebra, connected to the jaw, which slides up and down when you talk.

troy weight – as in, "Let's get going. I don't want to make ———."

truant – as in, "Is it ——— that Uncle Henry used to be the town drunk?"

trumpet – a harlot.

truncheon – a meal, usually eaten in the middle of the day.

trunnion – a game fish which, at certain seasons, comes up onto the shore to spawn.

trysail – what you do before you are forced to start the auxiliary engine.

tuba – as in, "So saying, he gave the ——— squeeze, and toothpaste shot all over the room."

tubby – as in, "Seeing the ——— immediately divorced himself of his attire and jumped in."

tuck – as in, "I got here first because I ——— the short cut."

Tudor – as in, "And so, rudely, she sat in the car and began to ——— horn at him."

Tuesday – the day between One's day and Three's day.

tulip – as in, "Man, you'll never get any high notes that way. You've got ——— them up there."

tumor – as in, "Is this a ——— is it just an empty pyramid?" Also, as in, "Bartender, we'll have ———."

tune – as in, "Yes, we'd like a table for ——— some coffee while we're waiting to order."

tungsten – as in, "Her ——— more damage than any of his so-called drinking problems."

tunic – as in, "Why are you whistling that weird ———?"

tunnel – as in, "No, the barn's nearly full so I think a ——— be enough."

Turk – a young turkey.

turkey trot – an intestinal disorder, common after Thanksgiving.

turnip – as in, "Well, Sergeant. Did you ——— any new leads?"

turnpike – something you do when barbecuing this great game fish."

turnstile – as in, "Yes, it's amazing how with this new business my husband ——— into dollars."

Tuscan – as in, "An elephant's bite may not hurt you, but his ———."

tutor – as in, "Shall I give the horn a ——— do we just wait here forever while she makes up her mind what to wear?"

tutti-frutti – a gay trumpet player.

tweak – a terrible week!

twoscore – pertaining to sexual success by two persons.

typhoid – used to be a baseball player down at the high school.

Tyrolese – as in, "Let's hike so fast we ——— kids out. Then we can ditch them and go for a beer!"

tzar – as in, "Excuse me, but those ——— our seats that you're sitting in!"

tzetze – as in, "Garcon, you may ——— wine down here."

U

U-boat – as in, "Hey, is thatta ———?" (Italian)

udder – as in, "After this the meeting collapsed into ——— chaos."

ulcer – a town in Ireland.

Ulyssean – as in, "Jethro, are ——— to me?"

umpire – as in, "Chief say, you likum mince pies; we break into bakery and get———."

unanimous – as in, "Well, my child, ——— take good care of you if she brings you to the park every day."

unaware – as in, "Oh my God, the gold is gone. Did you tell some——— we kept it hid?"

uncanny – having no toilet.

unction – an auction conducted by your uncle.

undercarriage – as in, "Chief say, Indian not want to attack, so why is white man hiding ———?"

underexpose – to show one's underwear.

underling – as in, "No, you are misinformed. During this dynasty the Chinese people enjoyed his rule, and were very happy ———."

undermine – as in, "Harriet, did you put your golf clubs ———?"

understand – to stand under something.

undertake – to not accept as much as you could actually have.

underwriter – one who writes under water.

uneasy – words which do not contain the letter 'E'.

unexpressed – when your pants have not been pressed by your ex-wife.

unheard – as in, "I'm afraid that some——— us getting in here."

unholy – without holes.

unicorn – one single kernel of maize.

unit – as in, "Tell me, Mrs. Clodhoppper, do ———?"

unite – as in, "Well, Baby, this is a ———." (Italian)

united – as in, "Parson, did you ——— and Mary in matrimony?"

universe – a poem with one stanza.

unprepared – not having previously had the skins removed. (pertaining to apples)

unprincipled – a school with no headmaster.

unravel – music which was not written by this distinguished composer.

unruly – not wanting to govern, usually refers to kings and presidents.

unseat – as in, "Howdy, Miz Purdy. Did you——— dinner yet?"

unsettle – as in, "If you——— little cheaper you'd have some money left over at the end of the month."

unshorn – having no shore.

unsightly – having no sights. (pertaining to rifles)

unstack – as in, "Say, kids, did you——— this dirty picture up on the wall?"

unsung – as in, "Say, have you——— that horse stealin' varmint yet?"

unweave – as in, "Well, Sheriff, they all got away except this ——— been holdin' here for you."

upholster – as in, "——— who works for Gallup polls told me that 70 percent of the American people still think that the world is flat. The rest think that the world is square."

upper – as in, "I think that my wife wants to look ——— old friends while we're here in town."

up-to-date – as in, "Hey, man, you've really got to be ——— a chick like this!"

Ural – as in, "Okay, freeze! ——— under arrest."

urchin – as in, "Why do you want to date a girl who has a big wart on ———?"

urine – as in, "Is this bowl ——— or is it mine?"

Ursa Major – as in, "What did ——— in up at State College?"

usage – as in, "No, you idiot. You don't flavor a chicken with cloves! ———."

use – as in, "Hey, ——— guys, are youse comin'?"

usher – as in, "Shay, ish that lady winking at ——— not."

V

vacancy – an ocean with nothing in sight.

vagabond – as in, "Now, let me get this straight. A hobo came to the door, and you didn't have any money. So you went to our safe and you gave that ———?"

vagrant – a poorly defined endowment or gift of money.

valet – a depression between hills or mountains.

valor – as the queen's mother said, "Are you gonna stay with this Prince —— are you coming home with me?"

value – as in, "If you stay with —— will never have anything. He'll always be riding off on some crusade or other."

vampire – an umpire for vamps.

variance – as in, "This reminds me of the last picnic I was on. We were overrun with ants, in fact I think they were these ——."

various – as in, "Now, I like this picture, it's ——."

vase – as in, "No, I don't remember your name, but your —— is familiar."

vaseline – as in, "When the feudal lord increased his obligation, and took away his food supplies, that's what made his ——."

vein – empty, unmeaning, or devoid of real value.

veldt – as in, "I —— a strange feeling come over me, which I —— I had never —— before."

velvet – as in, "——, vot seems to be the trouble vis mine pussycat?"

vend – as in, "She picked herself up and —— on her vay."

vendetta – as in, "Now I ask you, be sensible. —— girl who looks like that ever say 'yes' to a guy who looks lika you?"

veneer – as in, "Vy do you vant to leave home, —— you have everything you need?"

venison – as in, "Ach, how times have changed, —— says dot to his poor old fadder."

ventilate – as in, "I turned on the air conditioning, but your son opened the —— and we nearly roasted to death."

venture – as in, "Penelope, go open the ——— father installed on the furnace."

venue – as in, "Okay, Sveetheart, ——— come to your senses and don't think you're such a big deal, den you call old Hans, ja?"

veranda – a girl's name.

verbose – as in, "Ja, ve ——— in bed, und der house began shaking, mit der dishes knocking und der plaster falling. I tell you, it vas awful."

verdure – as in the song, "——— like to swing on a star? Carry moonbeams home in jar?"

verify – as in, "Und den I vas in a position ——— vent forward on the ledge I vould fall into the canyon, und if I vent backward der mountain katzen vould scratch mine behind."

verity – as in, "I dreamed I vas in a big palace ——— vas being served. Und everybody vas dressed up in fine clothes, but me, I didn't haf no clothes on."

vermin – as in, "Herr grocer man, der ist a ——— mine apple here!"

veronica – girl who played her harmonica on the beach at Santa Monica.

versed – as in, "Ja, ja, I need to get some sleep, but ——— a little supper, ja?"

versus – as in, "Frankly, these ——— are a bunch of trash."

vertigo – as in, "I know he came in here, now ———, huh?"

very – as in, "Tell me. I vant to know ——— vent."

vesper – as in, "Shhh, the congregation is praying. Ve'll haf to talk in a ———."

vest – as in, "Ja, ve like it out here in der ———, mit der sun shining; und no snow und ice to freeze us und give us der cold feets."

vesture – as in, "I think dot out here in der ——— all a bunch of veirdos."

veto – as in, "Und dot is vy ——— dis car all der vay here from Lodi."

via – as in, "Gootby, gootby, ——— going now."

viaduct – as in, "Freda, I told you I vanted a goose for Christmas, so ——— huh?"

vial – low, degraded or cheap.

vicar – as in, "She and ——— coming over this evening for a game of leapfrog."

vice – something which belongs to Violet.

viceroy – as in, "No, I can't marry you because you're too fond of ———."

vicious – something you catch in a German stream.

victim – as in, "I should he———, but I don't have the heart."

victory – a king's man named Victor.

viking – as in, "———, I never knew you could be so playful."

vile – as in, "——— this fuss. Let's chust hang him und get it over vith."

villa – as in, "Ja, but ——— rich girl, mit all kinds of chewels und stoff vant to marry a poor dumb clod like dot?"

vine – as in, "You come over den, mit der vife, at seven den. Dot vould be ———."

vinyl – as in, "If you don't cut back your grapes this season the ——— grow clear over your house by next year."

violate – as in, "I learned to play the bass ——— in life, and it was often my greatest delight to sit up most of the night, sawing away, and driving the other tenants of the building slowly mad."

vicious

violent – as in, "No, I can't play any gigs this weekend, man. I have my bass ———— out to the symphony until Thursday."

violin – as in, "You look positively ———— that nauseous green dress, my dear."

viper – something which a Mercedes Owners' Manual tells you keeps the rain off the windshield.

virgin – as in, "I can sit in this meeting no longer. What you are suggesting, Sir, is ———— on treason."

virginhood – an inexperienced crook.

virile – as in, "I'm getting tired now, so ———— I sleep?"

virtual – as in, "Her ———— never be betrayed."

viscount – as in, "————, vy are you looking at my neck dot vay? Und, you should see a dentist about dose teeth. Your bite is terrible, you need braces or something."

Vishnu – as in, "I ———— friends vould alvays be as nice as you."

vision – as in, "Don't try to shtop me Ingrid. I am goin' ————, und dot's dot."

visor – as in, "I can not understand ———— you vould vant to visit East Chermany."

visualize – as in, "Her make-up gives her very ————."

vixen – as in, "Und vith dis ve are ———— your clock, mister shmart guy."

volley – as in, "After he chumped over der ———— fell about three hundred feet straight into der sea. Der poor dumb cluck didn't know dot der castle vas built on a cliff."

volunteer – as in, "I know you are crying, Dollink, 'cause there is a little ———— on your cheek."

vortex – as in, "Vot did you do in der ————?"

vowel – as in, "Dis is a ———— deed dot you do, Herr Himmler."

vox – as in, "Vy are der hunds chasing dot ————?"

265

W

wad – as in the song, "——— a day this has been, ——— a rare mood I'm in . . . ."

wade – as in the song, "——— 'til the sun shines, Nellie ———."

wafer – as in, "I think it would be best if I went a ——— awhile."

waffle – as in, "Oh my goodness, how ———."

wagon – as in, "If that dog doesn't stop ——— his tail it'll fall off."

wainscot – as in, "Three fish aren't very many, ——— twelve already."

wainwright – as in, "He said I wouldn't get far with his sister, and boy, was ———."

waist – as in, "Spending six months on a desert island with you and just being friends seems like such a ———."

waive – as in, "Watch out for that big ———, Pop."

wallaby – as in, "I tried to talk to her, but for all the good it did me I might as ——— on the moon."

wallet – as in, "I've figured out what to do about that ugly pipe in the corner of the living room. Why don't we ——— up."

walleyed – as in, "I was really embarrassed at the dance last night, the way that guy by the ——— me all night."

walnut – someone who really loves walls.

walrus – as in, "Why did you knock that hole in my ———?"

waltz – as in, "Who the hell painted my ——— green?"

wan – as in, "Don ———" or "after ——— you're Don."

wander – as in, "I ——— why your father isn't home yet."

wane – a boy's name.

wanton – as in, "You can't blame her for —— to get out of here."

war – as in, "Where's that kangaroo costume you —— to the party last year?"

warble – a male bovine animal used in battle.

war club – the elite at the pentagon.

war cry – a sobbing because you can't go to the front lines.

ward – as in, "A little-known tribe, the Hottensnooks, lived in this area for many years, and continually —— upon their peace-loving neighbors."

warden – as in, "I saw —— the picture, 'How Red Was My Sunburn,' and he was lousy."

wardrobe – what an officer wears in the wardroom.

wardroom – as in, "All right, step back now and give —— to breathe."

ware – as in, "——, oh —— has my little dog gone."

warehouse – a question, as in, "—— that naughty ladies live in?"

warfare – as in, "I'm going to take my bazooka and go home. You fellows don't fight ——."

warlike – as in, "How did we ever get involved in a —— this?"

warlock – something on the door of the war room at the pentagon.

warpaint – as in, "The —— too bad, let's use this two-by-four anyway."

warren – as in, "I'm tired of all this talking. Let's make —— them dumb flatlanders!"

warsaw – as in, "This terrible —— friend fighting against friend, and brother against brother."

wartime – as in, "How can I ever get rid of this horrible —— carrying on my hand?"

washboard – a dull uninterested feeling caused by doing too much laundry."

washer – as in, "Take this little wildcat down to the creek and ——— off."

Washington – laundering two thousand pounds.

washwoman – as in, "Don't you think that before preparing our food you should at least ———?"

wassail – as in, "Uncle Popeye, ——— really more fun than steam?"

waste – as in, "Let me put my arm around your ——— my love."

wasteful – as in, "I can tell when I'm eating too much food because I get a ———."

watch chain – as Tarzan once said, "Boy want to learn how not to swing from tree, Boy ———."

watchmaker – as in, "I can't understand it. All I did was show her my new digital timepiece, and she ran screaming out of the house. Why would my ——— do that?"

watchtower – as in, "I know that all last week State College's spies ——— team go through practice."

water – as in, "I don't think her left hand knows ——— right is doing!"

Water Bearer – as in, "Is that a ——— is it just an oversized beaver?"

waterborne – something which happens only to infant whales.

watercourse – as in, "One of my required subjects in college was a ———."

water dog – something which happens when you're watering the lawn and Fido gets in the way. Also, as in, "I don't think she knows ——— did to poor old Mrs. Chumley."

waterfall – as in, "I've paid a few bucks for hairpieces, but I couldn't believe ——— cost her."

"Boy want to learn how not to swing
from tree. Boy watch chain."

waterfowl – as in, "I believe it was the pollution from the pig's knuckle plant up stream that made the ———."

water hemlock – as in, "I don't believe Mrs. Socrates knew ——— was being used for!"

water hole – as in, "No, don't distill it, you fool! I want this ———."

water jacket – as in, "Until she had it appraised, she didn't know ——— was worth."

Waterloo – a girlfriend of Napoleon's.

waterman – as in, "How about some whiskey and ———?"

water meter – as in, "She was going to drown herself in the ocean, but when she felt the ——— feet she decided it was too cold."

water moccasin – something which can happen to an Indian who is caring for his lawn.

water polo – as in, "Did Lady Smootley see ——— pony gave birth to last night?"

waterproof – as in, "I don't know ——— is, but she says she can crack this case wide open."

water spaniel – as in, "I don't care if she's upset. You oughta see ——— did to my new pants!"

watertight – as in, "I'm going to call her up and tell her ———fisted husband did to get out of paying for his share of the community clubhouse."

waterworks – as in, "If cleaning fluid won't get it out see if ———."

watt – as in, "——— the hell is that supposed to mean?"

wattle – as in, "Oh, ——— we do? Your father's lost his job, and the rent's due."

waver – as in, "What did you throw that pass my ———? I'm not an eligible receiver!"

wavy – as in, "With a show of bravado, and one final ———— jumped feet-first into the nearly frozen lake, only to reappear a moment later, gasping, and screaming for help!"

wax – the Women's Army Corps. Also as in, "So saying, he picked up a stout stick and gave the unfortunate lad 40 ————."

waxen – as in, "Hey, let's go roust those ———— the women's barracks."

waylay – as in, "I'll bet that when you stuck little Freddie with the pin you made him ————."

weak-kneed – as in, "I don't know what's going on! So far I have had six teenage girls in here who just this ———— their boyfriends in retaliation for what they said was obscene language."

wear – as in, "———— have you been, you rotten little sneak. Your father and I have been looking everywhere for you!"

weasel – as in, "Yes, it was a horrible wreck. The train was coming very fast, and I guess the driver of the car didn't hear the ————."

weather – as in, "I just thought that I'd call and see ———— I could come over after awhile."

weather-beaten – as in, "Sir, now that we can control tornadoes I think that we have the ————! If only we could do something about the General's halitosis!"

weathercock – as in, "I don't know ———— fighting is legal in this state or not."

weather strip – as in, "Well, here's our chance to find out ———— joints can operate in this city without police protection."

weave – as in, "I must confess, ———— just about had it with your stupid kid!"

wedgewood – as in, "No, an axe won't split that stump, but a ———— help!"

wedlock – what you secure your wife's chastity belt with.

weekend – as in, "I've been sitting around so much that I've developed a –––––."

weevil – as in, "This ––––– surely be the talk of the textile show this year."

weigh – as in, "I found a new ––––– to get here!"

welfare – making a meal out of tiny creatures which live in your well.

well-advised – having been told that you should drink only water from a spring.

well-born – having been born in a well.

well-bred – a hardened loaf of whole wheat which is hung in the well until it becomes soggy.

well-disposed – getting rid of someone by dumping them down a well.

well-groomed – a well which has been manicured or kept tidy.

well-grounded – a well with a lightning rod attached.

wellhead – an outhouse located over a well.

well-read – as in, "Hey, let's sneak over to Farmer Jones place and dye his –––––."

Welsh – as in, "Shay, this ––––– got nothing but water in it!"

wench – a tool for gripping and turning a nut.

werewolf – as in, "This is the kind of country ––––– packs abound."

westward – as in, "Why don't you go ––––– and leave me here in peace."

wet nurse – one who's caught in a sudden downpour on the way to the hospital.

whale – as in, "This cheese tastes all right, but one whiff of the ––––– knock you over."

wheelman – as in, "You'd better give me the ———! That's the third traffic cop who's had to run for safety."

wheeze – sounds heard coming from a roller coaster.

where – as in, "Keep punching champ. I think you're starting to ——— him down."

whereabout – as in, "Is there a place in your fine town ——— might be held between your champion and the Masked Marvel?"

wherefore – as in, "Do you realize that on the other side of this prison there's a building ——— hundred women are living. And here we are, locked up and helpless!"

whet – as in, "I wish this rain would stop. I'm getting ———"

whinny – as in, "He can be very helpful ——— wants to."

whippoorwill – as someone once said to Shakespeare, "Perhaps your wife would be more considerate of you if you ———."

whirl – as in, "This is the fourth town we've been throwed out of now, Zeke. ——— we go from here?"

whisker – as in, "I'm gonna grab that little gal and ——— right onto the dance floor."

whistle – as in, "As any card player can tell you, the game of ——— drive you crazy."

White House – as in, "Good morning Mr. ——— your crazy brother Albert today?"

white collar – as in, "My mother says to have Mrs. ———."

whole – as in, "Mommy, who put this ——— in my donut?"

wholesale – as in, "My wife spent the ——— buying so much stuff that I could hardly get it all into the car."

wholesome – as in, "What kind of a golf course is this? As soon as I dropped my ball into the ——— guy ran up, grabbed it, and threw it into a water trap."

wholly – as in, "Take off thy shoes for whereon thou standest is ——— ground."

whoopee – as in, "Witch doctor say, '——— on sacred drum?'"

whore – as in, "Tonight's Mystery Theater presents a tale of Gothic ———."

whose – sounds made by owls.

wicked – a lamp which has been newly trimmed.

widely – as in, "You"ll never hit the ball that way, you're swinging too ———."

widespread – as in, "Don't put that ——— on your twin bed."

wiener – as Captain Hook once said, "Neither ——— anyone else is ever going to get that treasure now."

wig – an adherent of the Presbyterian cause in Scotland.

wiggle – as in, "This ——— make you look twenty years younger!"

wight – an affirmative response, made by Porky Pig.

wigwag – a rogue who goes around snatching wigs.

wigwam – as in, "Here, put this hot coal on top of your head. That'll keep your ———."

wild – as in, "She ——— away the hours making lewd tapestries, which she hung in the courtyard."

wild fowl – a ball which ticks off the bat and goes spinning crazily off into the stands.

wildwood – hashish.

wile – as in, "I will not stand idly by ——— you speak thus of Her Ladyship!"

wilful – as in, "Boy is ——— of tricks. He just dropped little Miles down the well."

willow – as in, "——— Will, why aren't you here to protect me from the advances of this heathen scoundrel."

wince – as in, "In spite of what they say, it's not how you play the game! It's when one ——— that it counts!"

winch – a serving girl or rustic young woman.

Winchester – as in, "Good luck with the race, and I hope you ———."

windbreak – as in, "Have the kids been playing baseball again, or did the ——— this window?"

windjammer – as in, "As she rounded the corner of the building he saw the ——— frail body into a doorway."

windlass – as in, "Into the teeth of the roaring gale he shouted, how do you like this little ———?"

windy – as in, "Facing into the ——— spread his makeshift wings wide, and was immediately blown flat upon his rear."

winsome – as in, "Oh well, you ———, you lose some!"

winter – as in, "I ——— old man Murphy, and he said you was the one who put the pig in the church organ."

wire – as in, "There's work to be done here, so ——— you all standing around?"

wisdom – as in, "I went and saw the wizard, and boy, is the ———. He told me that if I wanted to get rid of these warts I should hold my hand in a bucket of warm cow manure for three days."

wise – as in, "——— that fellow painting his barn pink? I told you there's something odd about that family!"

witch hazel – as in, "My mother was right! You're a ——— and I never should have married you!"

wither – as in, "——— head stuck in the crockpot and still wearing the ape suit, she was easily one of the strangest figures I had ever seen!"

witness – as the chief said, "You're really a ———. Now can the stupid jokes, and get out there and nab Capone."

witty – as in, "Yes, he may want to live with her, but —— marry her?"

Woden – as in, "We —— wode, for just hours, and we still couldn't catch that dweadful person!"

woe – a command to a horse or mule, instructing it to stop.

wolfhound – as in, "He knows you're married, so what makes that —— you all the time?"

womb – as in, "Thith —— ith thertainly lovely, Clara."

wombat – as in, "We set fire to Count Dracula's castle, and now we've really got a ——."

woodchuck – as in, "—— mind if we borrowed his electric peanut pounder, Mrs. Martin?"

wooden – as in, "She —— say yes, and she —— say no."

woodenhead – an outhouse.

woodland – as in, "Where did that piece of —— that flew up when I split the log?"

woodlouse – as in, "Don't invite Herbert to the party. He —— everything up."

woodpecker – as in, "Every morning, as she took her sun bath, her perverted parrot —— unmercifully."

woodpile – as in, "I really like her pumpkin and mince pies, but her —— make you sick!"

woodside – as in, "I knew that Ethel —— with the boys. She'll do anything to get them to like her."

woodward – as in, "So, by this deception, we people of the valleys lived peacefully for many years, while the people of the —— among themselves."

woodwork – as in, "I really didn't think that it ——."

workable – to make use of a male bovine animal.

workwoman – as in, "We're going to have to put you to —————."

wormhole – as in, "Don't break it into two parts, Daddy. I want the —————."

wormwood – as in, "I might have known that ————— be seeing another woman just as soon as my back was turned!"

wormy – as in, "I don't know what happened. We were going fishing, and then when he say my ————— just fainted away."

worse – as in, " ————— so sorry that little Marvin can't come to the children's party this year."

worsted – as in, "And that's not the —————. After that, she said that you drank too much and ran around with other women."

worthy – as in, "————— less than thou art, I would still be thine."

wot – as in, "————— the hell do you kids think you're doin'?"

wrangle – the past tense of wrinkle.

wrecker – as in, "I told her that woman would eventually ————— marriage."

wrestle – as in, "You two can eat lunch now, the ————— have to wait until you're through."

wriggle – as in, "This ————— carry a load of over ten tons and do better than a hundred miles an hour."

wring – as in, "With this ————— I thee wed."

wrinkle – as in, "This ————— be finished in about two months; then we can go skating every day."

write – as in, "It's not that she's a bad girl, she just can't tell ————— from wrong."

writhe – as in, "Let uth ————— up and throw off thith wicked oprethor."

writing – anything made from rye flour.

wrought – as in, "If you don't go to the dentist soon your teeth are going to ——— right out of your head!"

wrung – part of a ladder that you step on.

wry – a type of grain.

X

xenia – as in, "I thought that I ——— coming out of the saloon yesterday, Preacher!"

xenon – as in, "Ladies, this is the same wonderful gadget that you have ——— our T.V. ads."

x-ray – as in, "Isn't that Peter out with your ———?"

xylophone – a telephone in an airproof tower used for storing grain.

y

yahoo – as in, "——— ist dot, talking on mine telephone?"

yak – a laugh.

Yankee – as in, "And then, medicine man ——— from my hand and drive new Cadillac into swamp!"

Yankeedom – an expression, indicating stupidity on our part, which is shared by many peoples of the world today.

yardstick – as in, "You're going to have to put glue under that plastic grass if you want to make your ——— together."

yawl – as in, "——— come back now, heah?"

yawn – as in, "What say we have some sport with——— fair maiden."

yearn – as in, "No, you dummy. This one is ———, and that one's mine."

yellowtail – a story about a coward.

yew – as in, "——— are certainly asking fer trouble, young feller!"

yokel – as in, "Yumpin' yimmy, this ——— really make the fellers down at the lodge laugh."

yon – an involuntary opening of the mouth to draw in oxygen.

yonder – as in, "The story was so boring that while I only sat there and ——— father went to sleep."

youth – as in, "So, John Barleycorn, ———thought you could escape me, eh?"

Yucatan – a tanning of the skin caused by drinking too much homemade brew, made from the distilled juice of the desert yucca plant.

yucca – an expression of distaste.

Yule – as in, "——— have to excuse me, I'm feeling rather queer!"

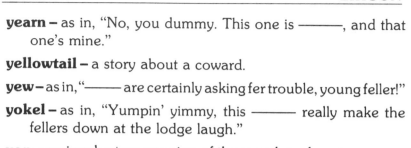

Z

zany – as in, "So ——— began writing western stories and signing his name, Zane Grey."

zebra – as in, "All right now, Madam. Take off ———."

zero – as in, "How do you like ——— of corn zat I have planted?"

Zeus – areas filled with wild animals and set aside for people to visit.

zinc – as in, "I ——— I vill go home now, yah?"

Zion – as in, "Don't just sit there ———. We've got to figure a way to get you out of this mess!"

zircon – a lesser-known knight in King Arthur's court once jailed for jousting in the nude.

zone – as in, "I haf——— up many rips in your pants, but never one this big!"

zoom – a zoo fully contained in one room.

zounds – as in, "Good heavens, where are those awful ——— coming from?"

Zulu – as in, "Would you like me to take you to the ——— ?"

zwieback – as in, "The middle period of time was called the Dark Ages, and that's——— in those days it was knight time!"

zweiback